GAME THEORY FOR EVERYDAY LIFE

A Practical Guide to Making Better Decisions at Work, in Relationships, and with Your Money (No Math Required)

Diego Gómez

Important Disclaimer: This book is for educational and entertainment purposes only. The author has made every effort to provide complete, accurate, current, and reliable information, but no guarantees can be made. The author is not an expert in legal, financial, medical, or professional advice. The information in this book has been compiled from various sources, so it is important that you consult a professional before trying any techniques described. By reading this book, you agree that the author is not responsible for any direct or indirect loss that may arise from the use of the information provided, such as errors or inaccuracies.

COPYRIGHT © Jaxbird LLC

Contents

Introduction 1

1. What Is Game Theory? 4

2. The Three Ingredients of Every "Game" 9

3. Rationality and Reality 15

4. Your First Strategic Decision 21

5. Thinking About What Others Think 26

6. The Prisoner's Dilemma 31

7. Nash Equilibrium: When Nobody
Wants to Change 36

8. Dominant Strategy: When There's a
Better Option 41

9. Zero-Sum and Positive-Sum 46

10. The Stag Hunt (The Risk of Trust) 51

11. The Focal Point: Coordinating
Without Words 56

12. Repeated Games 61

13. Information, Signals, and Commitments:
The Power of What's Credible 66

14. The Game of Chicken, or
Who Blinks First 71

15. Who Defines the Game: First
Mover Advantage and Anchoring 77

16. Positions and Interests 84

17. Escalation and De-escalation:
Getting Out of the Anger Game.............................90

18. When You Can't Win, Change the Rules........95

19. Game Theory in Relationships 101

20. Parents and Children: Incentives
and Tantrums..107

21. Friendships, Reciprocity, and Strategic
Forgiveness...114

22. Family, Inheritances, Coalitions,
and Christmas 121

23. Salary Negotiation and Interviews.................128

24. Colleagues and Teams: Allies or
Competition?...136

25. The Free Rider and the Tragedy of the
Commons (When Everyone Loses) 144

26. Mass Games: Voting, Auctions,
and Social Media 151

27. Habits, Procrastination, and Your
Future Self: Games with Yourself.......................159

28. Most Common Mistakes
and How to Avoid Them 167

29. Seven Strategic Questions 173

30. Infinite Games: When the Goal
is to Keep Playing 179

Appendix 1. The 10 Most Useful Games 185

Appendix 2. Biases That Sabotage
Your Decisions 194

About the Author 203

Introduction

This book was born from frustration.

For years I read about game theory in academic texts, and every time I finished with the same feeling: I understood the concepts in the abstract but had no idea what to do with them when my boss asked me to do something unfair, when my brother and I couldn't agree on what to do with our parents' house, or when a salesperson pressured me to close a deal I wasn't comfortable with.

The books explained the Prisoner's Dilemma with hypothetical criminals in interrogation rooms. Very interesting. But no one told me what to do on Tuesday at three in the afternoon when a colleague took credit for my work in front of the director.

So I decided to write the book I wish I'd found.

This isn't an economics or mathematics text. There are no equations, graphs, or formal proofs. What you'll find are situations you'll recognize: salary negotiations, arguments with your partner, family conflicts, work decisions, moments where what you get depends not only on what you do, but on what others decide to do.

Game theory, stripped of its intimidating jargon, is simply this: a way of thinking about situations where your outcome depends on other people's decisions. It sounds obvious when you put it that way. But most people make important decisions as if they were alone in the universe, considering only their own options without anticipating how their environment will react.

Each chapter presents an idea and grounds it in concrete examples. Some concepts have technical names worth knowing because they help you recognize patterns. Others are simply ways of thinking that, once you see them, you can't unsee.

My commitment is not to complicate what can be simple. If a concept requires a PhD to understand, it's not in this book. If an idea has no practical application in a normal person's life, it's not here either.

What you will find is a shift in perspective. Situations that seemed confusing before will begin to reveal their structure. Behaviors you once attributed to malice or stupidity will start to make sense when you understand the incentives that produce them. And your own decisions, I hope, will improve.

Not because you're going to become an infallible strategist. No one is. But because you'll see more clearly the terrain where you're operating.

1. What Is Game Theory?

You're at the grocery store in a hurry. Ahead of you, two checkout lanes: one with three people carrying light baskets, another with a single person pushing an overflowing cart. You have thirty seconds to decide. The lane with fewer people seems like the obvious choice, but that lone shopper is carrying enough groceries to stock a small nuclear bunker. The three people in the other line could move quickly, or they could be the type who dig for coupons at the bottom of their purse while the cashier waits. Your decision doesn't just depend on what you do. It depends on how those strangers behave, the cashier's speed, whether someone will pay in cash counting out coins, and many other variables.

This is the essence of what academics call game theory.

The term is misleading. It evokes board games, dice, perhaps screens with pixelated characters. But game theory has little to do with entertainment and everything to do with daily life. Its subject of study is simple yet profound:

how we make decisions when the outcome depends not only on us, but also on what others decide to do. Game theory could just as well be called "the science of interdependence."

Think about what to have for breakfast tomorrow. That decision is yours and yours alone. Whether you prefer eggs or fruit, no one else influences the outcome. Now think about something different: you're going out to dinner with friends and you've agreed to split the bill evenly. Suddenly, what you order is no longer just your business. If everyone orders modest dishes and you order lobster, you win. If everyone orders lobster and you ordered a salad, you lose. Your best choice depends on what you expect others to choose.

That's the difference between a personal decision and a strategic decision. In the first, you optimize based on your preferences. In the second, you optimize based on your preferences and your predictions about others' behavior.

A brilliant mathematician (John Nash) formalized these ideas decades ago, and his story made it to the movies, though the details of his personal life overshadowed his intellectual contribution. What matters here is that he didn't invent anything new. He simply put into equations something humans have practiced since they existed: anticipating others to decide better. You do it constantly without calling it by any technical name.

You negotiate with your partner about who washes the dishes tonight. If you think they'll give in because they're in a good mood, you stand firm. If you suspect there's no wiggle room today, you offer a trade. Before a job interview, you decide whether it's better to speak first to anchor the conversation or wait to adapt your response to what the interviewer reveals. On public transport, you choose a seat considering where passengers boarding after you might sit, seeking to maximize your personal space. Each of these situations is a small strategic game. And you play them well or poorly depending on how accurate your predictions are.

The good news is that this book won't turn you into a mathematician. There are no formulas to memorize, no graphs to decipher, no exams to pass. What can happen, if you pay attention and practice, is that you develop something like a sixth sense. An ability to look at everyday situations and perceive the hidden structure: who the real players are, what options each one has, what incentives drive them, and therefore what they might do. With that information, your own decisions will improve.

Let's return to the grocery store. The correct answer doesn't exist in the abstract. It depends on data you can quickly observe: the type of products in each cart, the attitude of people in line, the cashier's body language. But more important than the specific answer is the shift in mindset. You stopped seeing two lines. You started seeing a system where your outcome depends on variables you only partially control.

Now try this: before the day ends, identify three decisions where what you obtained depended on another person. It could be something insignificant, like who spoke first in a conversation, or something weightier, like a negotiation at work. The goal isn't to analyze each one, just to notice them. The first step to playing any game better is realizing you're playing.

And that's exactly what we'll do throughout these pages: learn to see the invisible games that structure your relationships, your work, your money, and your days. A game, in the sense we'll use here, is any situation where your best decision depends on what you think others will do. Once you see it, you can't unsee it.

2. The Three Ingredients of Every "Game"

A couple is debating where to have dinner. He wants sushi, she wants tacos. The conversation seems simple: two people, two preferences, pick one. But beneath that simple surface are three layers that neither of them is seeing, and these invisible layers will determine whether the night ends well or in uncomfortable silence.

The first layer is obvious: the players. In this case, him and her. But if you look more carefully, other participants emerge. The sushi restaurant closes early, so time is also playing. She had a difficult day at work, so her emotional state enters the scene. He gave in the last time they chose, and that history influences things now. The visible players are two, but the real players—the forces that affect the outcome—are more.

The second layer is strategies. He can insist, give in, propose a third place, or suggest they each eat separately tonight. She has the same options. But there are less obvious strategies: postpone the decision until hunger forces them to choose anything, delegate the choice to a random app, or change the question entirely with a "what if we cook together?" The real options always exceed those that first come to mind.

The third layer is outcomes. It seems like the only thing at stake is eating sushi or tacos. But for him, perhaps what's at stake is feeling that his preferences matter. For her, maybe what's relevant is not repeating the pattern of always giving in. For both, the peace of the evening is worth more than the specific menu. The real outcome isn't the restaurant chosen, but how they feel after choosing it.

Every strategic game, from a couple's dinner to a million-dollar negotiation, has exactly these three components: players, strategies, and outcomes. Recognizing them transforms confusing situations into navigable maps.

Players are those who have the capacity to influence the outcome. Sometimes they're obvious: you and your boss negotiating a raise, you and a seller haggling over price. But often the most important players remain hidden. When you accept a job, the labor market is a silent player that defines your bargaining power. When you decide how much to save this month, your future self is a player whose interests you should represent. Before acting in any situation, it's worth asking: who else has influence here that I'm not considering?

Strategies are the complete menu of possible actions, not just those that jump out at you. Facing a conflict with a colleague, the obvious options are confront or avoid. But there are others: wait for the problem to dissolve on its own, seek a mediator, redefine the relationship so the point of conflict stops mattering, or accept the situation and adjust your expectations. As illogical as it may seem, the strategy of doing nothing is a strategy. So is changing the entire game. Good players see doors where others only see walls.

Outcomes are what each player gains or loses based on the combination of decisions. And here's the most common mistake: assuming the outcome is measured only in obvious terms, in black and white or shades of gray. In a salary negotiation, it seems like the only thing that matters is the final number. But also at stake is your relationship with your boss, your reputation as someone reasonable or difficult, your own sense of worth, and the precedent you set for future conversations. Sometimes the person who "wins" the number loses something more valuable. Asking yourself what's really at stake—beyond the visible object of the dispute—radically changes how you play.

There's a simple tool that helps organize these three layers. You can call it the game map. It consists of drawing mentally—or on paper, if the situation warrants it—three columns. In the first, you list all the relevant players, including the hidden ones. In the second, you write down each player's real options, including the non-obvious ones like waiting, delegating, or changing the rules. In the third, you identify what outcomes genuinely matter to each party: not just the tangible ones, but also the emotional, relational, and reputational ones. Once you have that map in front of you, decisions become clearer. You know who you're playing with, what cards each one holds, and what's really being lost or gained.

The couple we mentioned at the beginning never did this exercise. They argued for twenty minutes about sushi versus tacos, when the real game was something else: he needed to feel his voice counted, she needed not to feel ignored after an exhausting day. If they had mapped the situation correctly, they would have discovered they both wanted the same thing: a peaceful evening where both felt good, and that the specific restaurant was almost irrelevant. They ended up ordering pizza at home, both frustrated. Not because the pizza was bad, but because they arrived at it through exhaustion rather than by design.

Think now about a decision you have pending. Before moving forward, take five minutes to map it. Write down who the real players are, including any hidden forces that influence things. List each one's options, especially the less obvious ones like not acting or even changing the rules of the game. And finally, identify what's truly at stake for each party. This simple exercise, which takes no more than a few minutes, will give you a clarity that most people never have when making important decisions.

Before deciding, always ask yourself: Who's playing? What can each one do? What do we really care about? The answers to those three questions are the ground on which good decisions are built.

3. Rationality and Reality

Someone offers you ten dollars for free. The only condition is that another person, a stranger, decides how to split them between you both. That person looks at you and makes their offer: one dollar for you, nine for them. You can accept and keep your dollar, or reject it and both of you leave with nothing. One free dollar or zero. From any mathematical angle, the answer is obvious: accept. Something always beats nothing.

But something in you rebels. The offer feels like a slap in the face. That person has just told you, without words, that your acceptance is worth less than a dollar. That they can keep ninety percent because they assume you'll swallow whatever crumbs they throw you. And suddenly, rejecting and walking away with nothing feels better than accepting and feeling humiliated. You'd rather lose the dollar as long as they lose their nine.

This scenario has a name: the ultimatum game. And what it reveals about humans contradicts almost everything classical economics assumed about us.

If we were the purely rational creatures that traditional models imagined, we'd accept any positive offer. One cent is better than zero cents. End of analysis. But when researchers put real people in this situation, they discovered something different. Most reject offers below thirty percent. There's a threshold below which money stops mattering and what matters is the message. Accepting an insulting offer feels like validating the insult, and that hurts more than losing a few bills.

The practical implication is enormous. Every time you interact with another person in a strategic situation, you have two options: play with the logical robot that theory describes, or play with the real human being in front of you. The robot would accept any positive offer, respond only to numerical incentives, and never make decisions based on pride or revenge. The real human will do things that seem irrational from the outside but have perfect logic from the inside. They'll reject advantageous deals because they felt disrespected. They'll pay high costs to punish what they perceive as injustice. They'll sacrifice their own gains just so the other person doesn't gain as much.

This means your offers, proposals, and negotiations must pass two filters: the logic filter ("does it make numerical sense?") and the emotional filter ("how will the other person feel receiving it?"). A perfectly rational proposal that humiliates the recipient will be rejected. A less optimal proposal on paper that preserves the other person's dignity has a better chance of being accepted.

Emotions aren't noise interfering with strategic decisions. They're part of the game itself. And emotions come accompanied by predictable biases. Overconfidence makes you overestimate your abilities and underestimate obstacles: you think the project will take two weeks when it'll take six, that the negotiation will be easy when it'll be brutal, that you're right when you only have a partial perspective. Loss aversion makes the pain of losing something weigh more than the pleasure of gaining the same thing: you'll work harder to avoid losing a hundred dollars than to gain a hundred dollars, even though mathematically they're equivalent. Herd thinking pushes you to do what others do, assuming that if everyone's going in that direction they must know something you don't, when often they're just following someone who doesn't know either. Confirmation bias makes you seek information that confirms what you already believe and ignore what contradicts it, building a reality tailored to you that can be dangerously removed from actual reality.

These biases aren't defects you can eliminate through willpower. They're part of the mental equipment you were born with. What you can do is know them, anticipate when they'll appear, and adjust your decisions knowing that your perception is filtered.

Now, here's an important twist. Sometimes what seems irrational from the outside has internal logic. Rejecting the dollar in the ultimatum game seems foolish if you only look at the money. But if you look at dignity, self-respect, or the message you're sending about how you expect to be treated, the decision makes sense. Many actions that others (or you yourself) label as irrational are protecting something that doesn't appear in the visible equation: a principle, an identity, a line you're not willing to cross.

Think about some past decision where your emotions led you to act in an apparently irrational way. Perhaps you rejected an offer that suited you, or paid a high price to make a point, or chose the difficult path when the easy one was available. Before judging yourself, ask what else was at stake. Sometimes you'll discover you were protecting something real: your dignity, your principles, your sense of who you are. And other times you'll discover that a bias played a trick on you. Distinguishing between these cases is part of the work of thinking strategically.

Perfect rationality, that creature that coldly calculates each move without emotions affecting it, is a useful myth for building theoretical models but nonexistent in the real world. Good strategists don't try to become robots. They know they themselves are subject to biases and emotions, and they know their counterparts are too. They use that knowledge to predict better, to design proposals that work with real humans, and to avoid the most common mental traps. The advantage isn't in eliminating emotions from the game—that's impossible—but in understanding them well enough so they work in your favor instead of against you.

4. Your First Strategic Decision

You want to start going to the gym. The problem is you hate crowds, and the gym at six in the evening looks like a can of sardines with exercise equipment. Your reasoning is simple: if everyone goes at six, your best option is to go at seven in the morning, when the place will be empty. Perfect. Except you're not the only one who hates crowds. If enough people think exactly like you, seven in the morning will become the new peak hour, and your brilliant strategy will leave you surrounded by people in tights doing exactly what you were trying to avoid.

Your best decision depends on what you think others will do. But what others do depends on what they think you'll do. And so the dance begins.

This is the heart of strategic thinking: the best response. Given what you expect the other party to do, your best response is the option that maximizes your outcome under that expectation. It sounds abstract, but you apply it constantly without naming it. When you decide what time to leave home to avoid traffic, you're making a prediction about how many other people will leave at that same time and choosing your moment based on that. When you choose what topic to propose for a project at work, you consider what topics your colleagues will propose and seek to differentiate yourself or complement them.

Basic strategic thinking follows a structure: if I do X and they do Y, then the result will be Z. What distinguishes a good strategist from a mediocre one is the quality of that prediction about Y. It's not enough to know what you want to do. You need to anticipate the environment's reaction to your action.

There are two common errors that sabotage this process. The first is deciding as if you were alone. You focus on your preferences, analyze your options, and choose the one you like most, forgetting that the final outcome doesn't depend only on you. It's like choosing a restaurant for a date thinking only about what you want to eat, without considering that the other person also has preferences and that ignoring them has consequences. The second error is assuming others are statues: that they'll do what they always do, without adjusting to what you do. If you publicly announce that you're going to start arriving early to meetings to take the best seat, don't be surprised when others start doing the same.

In traffic, this dynamic unfolds every day. You see two lanes: one seems to be moving faster, so you switch. But many others saw the same thing and switched too. Now the lane that was fast is slow, and the one you abandoned flows better. Your decision was rational given your prediction, but your prediction ignored that others would make the same reading. Something similar happens at parties and social events. If you calculate arriving late to avoid that awkward moment of being the first one there, consider that many others have the same calculation. That's how you get those parties where no one arrives until an hour after the stated time, because everyone was waiting for others to arrive first.

At work, choosing a project topic is a strategic decision disguised as a personal preference. If you propose something popular that several colleagues also want, you'll compete for resources and attention. If you propose something no one else considered, you'll have a clear field but perhaps less support. Your best topic depends on what topics others will propose, and that requires knowing them well enough to predict their moves.

Now, there's a special situation where the best strategy is precisely not to be predictable. If your opponent can anticipate exactly what you'll do, they'll use that information against you. A negotiator who always gives in to pressure will be pressured relentlessly. A competitor who always responds by lowering prices will be provoked into a price war. In these cases, introducing variability in your behavior—sometimes giving in, sometimes resisting, with no clear pattern—can be optimal. If they can't predict you, they can't exploit you.

This doesn't mean acting randomly at all times. Most everyday situations benefit from consistency and predictability: they build trust, facilitate coordination, allow others to count on you. But when you're in a genuinely competitive context, where the other party seeks to take advantage of any pattern they detect, being unpredictable stops being a defect and becomes an advantage.

The next time you face an important decision, before acting, complete this sentence in writing: if I do this, they'll probably do that, and then the result will be this other thing. You don't need certainty. It's enough to make your prediction explicit to realize whether it's reasonable or whether you're ignoring how the environment will react. Many decisions that seem difficult become clearer when you force your mind to complete that sequence.

Your best move doesn't exist in a vacuum. It's always the best response to what you expect others to do. Change your expectation about them and your best option changes too. That's why thinking strategically requires two mutually reinforcing skills: knowing your own options with clarity, and predicting others' actions with realism. Without the second, the first is an incomplete exercise.

5. Thinking About What Others Think

Imagine a simple contest. One hundred people each choose a number from one to one hundred. The winner is whoever gets closest to two-thirds of the average of all the numbers chosen. You have thirty seconds to decide. What number do you choose?

If you don't think about others, you'll probably choose something close to fifty: the midpoint, a safe bet. But if you think a bit more, you realize that many will choose numbers near the center. If the average is around fifty, two-thirds of that is approximately thirty-three. So you choose thirty-three to win. Except if others also reason this way, they'll also choose thirty-three, which makes that number the new average. Two-thirds of thirty-three is twenty-two. So maybe you should choose twenty-two. But if others reach that same conclusion...

This game illustrates something fundamental about strategic thinking: there are levels of depth, and most people don't get past the first one.

At level zero, you don't think about others. You choose what seems reasonable in isolation. At level one, you consider what others will do and adjust your decision accordingly. At level two, you think about what others believe you'll do, and adjust again. Each additional level adds a layer of reflection: I think that they think that I think that they think. In theory, this reasoning can continue indefinitely. In the two-thirds game, taken to its logical conclusion, everyone should choose zero. But in practice, almost no one gets that far.

This dynamic appears constantly outside of numerical contests. When you negotiate a price, you don't just think about how much the object is worth to you. You also think about how much the seller believes you're willing to pay. And if you're shrewd, you think about what the seller believes you think about their minimum acceptable price. He knows that you know the initial price is inflated. You know that he knows you know. The real negotiation happens several levels below the words being spoken.

In a job interview, preparing your answers is level one. Anticipating the difficult questions the interviewer might ask is level two. Preparing for the questions they'll ask precisely because they expect you won't be prepared is level three. In an argument with someone who knows you well, your obvious arguments will be anticipated and countered before you present them. The advantage lies in preparing the arguments that person doesn't expect you to use, precisely because they know you and think they can predict you.

But here's a trap: thinking too many levels ahead can distance you from reality instead of bringing you closer. If you're playing the two-thirds contest with a group of people who've never heard of game theory, choosing zero would be a colossal mistake. You'd win if everyone reasoned like you, but no one will. The actual average will be much higher, and your sophisticated choice will end up ridiculously far from the target. Excess strategic thinking can be as costly as a lack of it.

The practical key is to correctly calibrate your counterpart. You need to estimate what level of depth the other person operates at and position yourself one level above, not ten. If you're negotiating with someone who hasn't thought much about the matter, anticipating three moves ahead is a waste of energy. If you're negotiating with an experienced professional, staying at the superficial level will leave you exposed. The art is in reading your opponent and adjusting your depth of analysis to theirs.

This requires a skill that isn't taught in any manual: observing people and calibrating their strategic sophistication. Some signals help. Someone who asks questions about your motivations is probably thinking at deeper levels than someone who only talks about their own needs. Someone who mentions hypothetical scenarios is mentally simulating your possible responses. Someone who seems one step ahead in the conversation probably is.

The next time you face an important decision involving another person, before acting, ask yourself what that person expects you to do. Ask yourself that question explicitly, not just as a vague intuition. And once you have an answer, consider whether doing something different would give you an advantage. Sometimes the best move is exactly what they expect you to do. But sometimes, knowing what they expect allows you to surprise them.

It's not enough to think about what others will do. The effective strategist thinks about what others believe they will do, and uses that information to decide better. The optimal depth isn't the maximum possible, but rather what matches the depth of whoever is in front of you.

6. The Prisoner's Dilemma

Two suspects. Two interrogation rooms. A detective in each one making the same offer.

You and your accomplice committed a crime together. You've been arrested, but the evidence is weak. If you both stay silent, they can only convict you on a minor charge: one year in prison for each of you. But the detective presents you with a tempting alternative. If you rat out your accomplice and he stays silent, you walk free today and he gets ten years. Of course, if he rats you out while you stay silent, the roles reverse: he walks free and you spend a decade locked up. And if you both rat each other out, you both get five years.

The detective closes his folder and looks at you. Your accomplice is receiving exactly the same offer in the room next door. You have to decide now, with no way to communicate with him.

You start calculating. If your accomplice stays silent, your options are clear: stay silent and get one year, or rat him out and walk free. Ratting him out is better. Now suppose your accomplice rats you out. Your options change: stay silent and get ten years, or rat him out too and get five. Ratting him out is still better. No matter what your accomplice does, ratting him out always improves your individual situation.

Your accomplice, in the other room, does exactly the same calculation. And reaches the same conclusion.

You both rat each other out. You both get five years. If you had cooperated by staying silent, you would have gotten only one. Each person's individual rationality produced a collective outcome that both hate. Neither did anything illogical. Both chose their best option given what the other could do. And yet, both lost.

This is the trap of the Prisoner's Dilemma: when distrust rules, individual logic destroys collective benefit. And this trap doesn't just live in hypothetical interrogations. It appears disguised in everyday situations constantly.

Two companies compete in the same market. Each could maintain reasonable prices and earn healthy profits. But if one lowers prices while the other maintains them, the first steals customers. So both lower them. And lower them more. And keep lowering until neither makes money, but they can't raise prices without handing customers to the competition. Both are trapped in an equilibrium that neither wants but that neither can escape alone.

Two neighboring countries could live in peace with minimal militaries. But if one arms itself while the other doesn't, the armed one gains power. So both arm themselves. Military budgets grow, resources get diverted from schools and hospitals, and both countries end up equally vulnerable as before but much poorer. The arms race is a Prisoner's Dilemma played with tanks and missiles.

Two roommates share a kitchen. Each would prefer the other to wash the dishes. If one stops washing them, the other might give in and do it all. But the other applies that same logic. Soon there's a mountain of dirty dishes that neither wants to touch, and both eat from disposable containers cursing in silence. Cooperation would have taken five minutes a day. Mutual defection generates an uninhabitable kitchen.

The Prisoner's Dilemma explains why groups of intelligent people end up with stupid outcomes. It's not that they're irrational. It's that the structure of the game turns individual rationality into a collective trap. Each person acts correctly given their incentives, and the result is that everyone loses.

There's a question that should be forming in your mind: if this pattern is so common and so destructive, is there any way out? The answer is yes, but it requires changing the conditions of the game. It requires finding ways to create trust, establish verifiable commitments, or turn the one-time encounter into a repeated relationship where betraying today has costs tomorrow. All of that comes later. For now, what matters is recognizing the trap when it appears.

Think about your current life. Is there some situation where you and another person are trapped in mutual distrust, where both do what seems individually rational and both end up losing? It might be with a colleague, a family member, a neighbor. Identify that situation. And ask yourself if there's a way to break the cycle, to create the conditions for cooperation to be possible. There isn't always one. But sometimes the way out exists and simply no one proposed it.

When distrust rules, everyone loses even though each person acts rationally. This is the central paradox of social life. And recognizing it is the first step to escaping it.

7. Nash Equilibrium: When Nobody Wants to Change

Two cars arrive at the same time at an intersection without a traffic light. Both drivers want to go. Both stop. Each watches the other, waiting for them to yield. Seconds pass. Nobody moves forward. Nobody backs up. One makes a motion to start and so does the other. Both hit the brakes again. The scene freezes in a stalemate we've all experienced.

What's curious isn't that nobody knows what to do. What's curious is that both know exactly what they want, both can see what the other wants, and yet neither can find a way to move without risk. It's not ignorance. It's a particular type of standoff where each person is waiting for the other, and precisely because of that, nothing changes.

This type of situation has a technical name that became famous: Nash equilibrium. And though it sounds like economist jargon, it describes something you'll recognize in dozens of moments in your life.

A Nash equilibrium occurs when everyone involved is doing the best they can given what the others are doing. No one can improve their situation by changing only their own decision, if the others maintain theirs. It doesn't mean everyone is happy. It doesn't mean it's the best possible outcome. It only means that no one has an incentive to move first.

Think about the routes you take to work. If there were a secret shortcut that nobody used, you'd take it and arrive faster. But shortcuts don't stay secret for long. Others discover them, use them, and the shortcut gets congested until it takes the same time as the other routes. At equilibrium, all viable alternatives take approximately the same time. If any were significantly faster, enough people would switch until that advantage disappeared. Traffic self-organizes into a state where no one can win by unilaterally changing routes.

This sounds efficient, but there are deeply unsatisfying equilibria. Remember the Prisoner's Dilemma from the previous chapter, where both suspects end up confessing even though they would have been better off if both had stayed silent. That mutual confession is a Nash equilibrium: neither can improve by changing only their decision. If you stay silent but the other confesses, your situation gets dramatically worse. So nobody changes. And the result is terrible for everyone.

That nobody wants to move doesn't mean everyone is satisfied. It means that moving alone is worse than staying put.

There's another interesting phenomenon: sometimes multiple equilibria are possible, and the difference between a good one and a bad one depends on how we coordinate. Consider which side of the road vehicles drive on. Everyone driving on the right works perfectly. Everyone driving on the left also works. What doesn't work is some choosing right and others left. Both options are stable equilibria, but getting to one or the other requires everyone to agree. Once established, no one wants to deviate.

Many everyday frustrations turn out to be disguised equilibria. The meeting that always starts late because everyone arrives late because they know the meeting always starts late. The team where nobody asks questions because nobody asks questions and silence seems normal. The family where certain topics are never touched because they've never been touched and breaking the pattern feels more costly than maintaining it. In each case, nobody changes because changing alone, without the others changing too, seems to make things worse.

But bad equilibria aren't eternal prisons. They can be broken.

Changing the rules works: if the meeting has consequences for arriving late, the individual incentive transforms. Communicating works: if someone says out loud that the dynamic of silence is uncomfortable, others can join in. Creating new incentives works: if asking questions in the team gets recognized instead of ignored, the equilibrium migrates to another point.

The intersection without a traffic light from the beginning has a solution. Someone installs a traffic light, or a yield sign, or simply the custom is established that the vehicle on the right has priority. Physical or social infrastructure solves the stalemate by converting an uncomfortable equilibrium into a functional one.

Now think about some situation in your life that seems immovable, something that's "always been this way" even though nobody likes it. Examine it through this lens: is each person doing what suits them given what the others are doing? If you changed alone, would you improve or get worse? If the answer is you'd get worse, you're probably trapped in an equilibrium. And if it's a bad equilibrium, the question is no longer why nobody changes, but what would need to be modified in the structure of the game for someone to want to move first.

An equilibrium isn't the best. It's just what nobody wants to change unilaterally. Recognizing this transforms frustration into diagnosis, and diagnosis is always a starting point from which to proceed.

8. Dominant Strategy: When There's a Better Option

You're offered a free umbrella. The sky is cloudy but there's no certainty of rain. You can take it or leave it. If it rains and you have it, you arrive dry. If it rains and you don't have it, you arrive soaked. If it doesn't rain and you have it, you're carrying a light object you didn't use. If it doesn't rain and you don't have it, nothing changes.

In three of the four scenarios, having the umbrella is equal to or better than not having it. In the fourth, it's dramatically better. There's no combination of circumstances where rejecting the umbrella leaves you in a better position than accepting it.

You've just found something valuable: a dominant strategy.

A dominant strategy is an option that wins no matter what happens around you. It doesn't depend on what others do, it doesn't depend on how events unfold, it doesn't require predicting the future or reading anyone's mind. It's simply better in all possible scenarios. When you find one, the decision stops being a decision. It becomes obvious.

The problem is that they're extraordinarily rare.

Most situations you face have that uncomfortable characteristic we've explored in previous chapters: your best option depends on what others choose. If your competitor lowers prices, maybe you should lower yours too. If your competitor maintains prices, maybe you can maintain yours. The right answer changes with the context. That's normal.

But occasionally an option appears that breaks that dependency. A move that works regardless of external variables.

Consider the decision to get vaccinated in the middle of an epidemic. If most of the population gets vaccinated, the disease circulates little and your vaccine gives you an extra layer of protection you might not even need. If few people get vaccinated, the disease circulates widely and your vaccine becomes your main defense. In both scenarios, being vaccinated leaves you in a better position than not being vaccinated. Others can do what they want; your optimal decision doesn't change.

Consider arriving prepared to a work meeting. If the meeting turns out to be important and there are tough questions, your preparation makes you look competent. If the meeting turns out to be trivial and nobody asks anything, you lost an hour preparing but you didn't look bad. There's no scenario where having arrived prepared hurts you. Preparation dominates improvisation in all possible combinations.

When you identify a genuine dominant strategy, the analysis ends. You don't need to weigh probabilities, you don't need to guess others' intentions, you don't need to calculate risks. The answer is clear and doubt is a waste of time.

But here comes the trap: many times we think we have a dominant strategy when we really don't.

The most common error is ignoring scenarios. An option seems to always win until someone points out a circumstance you hadn't considered. "Honesty is always best" sounds like a dominant strategy until you imagine situations where brutal honesty destroys a relationship you valued. "It's always better to save more" seems infallible until you consider the cost of missed opportunities from not investing or not enjoying life. Strategies that seem dominant at first glance frequently have cracks when you examine all possible scenarios.

The other error is confusing "generally better" with "always better." An option that wins ninety percent of the time is not a dominant strategy. It's a good bet, but it still depends on landing in that ninety percent. A true dominant strategy wins in one hundred percent of scenarios, including the improbable ones.

Before declaring you've found one, verify rigorously. List all relevant scenarios. For each one, confirm that your preferred option is at least as good as the alternatives. If you find a single scenario where another option would be better, what you have is not a dominant strategy. It's just a frequently good strategy that requires more careful analysis.

Now examine your own life. Is there any pending decision where one option is clearly superior regardless of what others do or how events unfold? If there genuinely is one, the interesting question is why you haven't taken it yet. Sometimes the answer is inertia. Sometimes it's that you hadn't done the analysis. And sometimes, when you think about it carefully, you discover it wasn't as dominant as it seemed.

When an option wins in all scenarios, don't think twice. That's your move. The clarity of a dominant strategy is a rare gift. When it appears, seize it.

9. Zero-Sum and Positive-Sum

He wants the beach. She wants the mountains. Vacation is in two weeks and they only have budget for one destination. The conversation starts cordial but quickly gets tense. Every argument for the beach feels like an attack on the mountains. Every defense of the mountains sounds like contempt for the beach. Both start grudgingly giving ground, calculating who has sacrificed more, keeping an invisible ledger of concessions. In the end they choose a place that excites neither of them, a geographic midpoint that half-satisfies and completely disappoints.

The trap they fell into was assuming only one could win.

There are situations where that's true. A chess board has a winner and a loser; the points you accumulate are exactly the points your opponent loses. A fixed inheritance gets divided among heirs; every dollar one receives is a dollar the others don't get. A job position with only one candidate selected means everyone else leaves without it. In these cases, the game is zero-sum: the total gain is predetermined and the only thing to decide is how it gets divided.

But most human interactions don't work that way.

When two people trade, both end up with something they value more than what they had before. You prefer the money to the object you're selling; the buyer prefers the object to the money they're paying. The transaction doesn't redistribute fixed value, it creates it. When two colleagues collaborate on a project, the result can be better than the sum of what each would have achieved separately. When a couple builds a life together, both can end up happier, more secure, and more fulfilled than they would have been alone. These are positive-sum games: it's possible for everyone to win simultaneously.

The most costly error in relationships and negotiations is confusing a positive-sum game with a zero-sum one. Treating every conversation as a battle. Assuming that if the other person gets something, you lose something. Defending your position tooth and nail because giving in feels like defeat. This mindset turns situations where both could win into wars where both lose.

The vacation couple fell into this. They assumed the pie was fixed: beach or mountains, one or the other, winner and loser. But before fighting over how to divide the pie, they could have asked themselves if it was possible to bake a bigger one.

What was he really looking for at the beach? Maybe rest, warmth, disconnection. What was she looking for in the mountains? Maybe fresh air, hiking, scenery. Is there a place that offers both? A coast with trails. A lake surrounded by mountains. An island with volcanoes. Suddenly the beach-versus-mountains conflict dissolves because it was never really about geography; it was about experiences they both wanted that weren't mutually exclusive.

Expanding the pie means looking for ways to create more value before arguing about how to divide it. In a salary negotiation, if the employer can't raise the number, maybe they can offer additional vacation days, flexible hours, or a different title. In a conflict between business partners about profit distribution, maybe they can first find ways to increase those profits. In a family dispute over who gets grandma's house, maybe they can explore whether one wants it to live in, another for vacations, and another simply wants liquidity, and design an arrangement that satisfies all three.

The transformative question is simple: is there any way for both of us to end up better than we started? If the answer is yes, then fighting over distribution before maximizing total value is a strategic error. First expand the pie. Then discuss the portions.

Before your next negotiation—whether with your boss, your partner, a seller, or a business partner—pause. Before defending your position, list three possible ways to expand the pie. Consider time: would changing deadlines help? Consider form: are there alternative ways to deliver the same thing? Consider conditions: what if we add or remove elements? Consider trades: is there something that costs you little to give but matters a lot for the other to receive?

That list can transform a confrontation into a collaboration.

Always ask yourself: is it possible for both of us to come out better than before? If the answer is yes, stop competing and start creating.

10. The Stag Hunt (The Risk of Trust)

Two hunters in a forest. Before them, an opportunity: a stag that would feed both families for weeks. The problem is that hunting it requires both of them. One must corner, the other must strike. If both coordinate, the prize is enormous. But on the way to the stag, each hunter passes by a hare. The hare is small, barely enough for a modest dinner, but it has one decisive advantage: you can catch it alone.

If your partner goes for the stag and you do too, you both eat abundantly. If your partner goes for the stag but you veer off toward the hare, you dine lightly and he gets nothing because he can't hunt the stag alone. And if both go for hares, each has his modest but guaranteed meal.

The temptation of the hare isn't greed. It's fear.

If you trust that the other will go for the stag and he follows through, you both win. But if you trust and the other fails you, you're left empty-handed. The hare protects you against that possibility. It's the consolation prize you can obtain without depending on anyone.

This scenario is known as the stag hunt, and it captures something different from the prisoner's dilemma we explored earlier. In the prisoner's dilemma, betrayal was tempting even if the other cooperated: you could gain more by ratting out a loyal accomplice than by staying silent. Here that temptation doesn't exist. If your hunting partner goes for the stag, the best thing for you is to go for the stag too. Nobody wants to betray. The problem is different: nobody knows for certain what the other will do, and the cost of being wrong is getting nothing.

The difference is subtle but crucial. In the prisoner's dilemma, the obstacle is the structure of incentives. In the stag hunt, the obstacle is trust.

Think about two people who decide to start a business together. The venture has enormous potential, but only if both commit completely. If both quit their secure jobs, invest their savings, and work tirelessly, the company can take off.

But if one gives everything while the other keeps their stable job "just in case," the half-hearted effort sinks the project. The person who bet everything loses their investment. The one who kept a foot out preserves their salary but kills the opportunity for both.

There's no ill intent. Each simply fears the other won't commit enough, and that fear makes protecting yourself seem reasonable. The result is that both choose hares when they could have hunted a stag.

The same thing happens when a couple considers moving in together. If both commit fully, they share expenses, build a home, deepen the relationship. But if one commits while the other keeps their apartment "just in case," the dynamic becomes poisoned. The one who bet everything feels exposed. The one who hedged never fully invests emotionally. The relationship stalls in a limbo that satisfies neither.

The pattern repeats in work teams, in business partnerships, in friendships where someone needs a big favor. Life's most valuable prizes require coordination, and coordination requires something that can't be forced: trust that the other will also go for the stag.

The tragedy is that many people spend their lives hunting hares. Not because hares are what they want, but because the stag requires exposure, and exposure is scary. The security of the small prize is more attractive than the vulnerability of the big one.

How do you build the trust necessary to go for stags? Sometimes with explicit words: conversations where both parties declare their intention and openly commit. Sometimes with costly signals: quitting the secure job first, signing the joint lease, doing something that demonstrates you don't have one foot out the door. Sometimes with gradual steps: small stags first, low-risk projects where they can test each other's reliability before betting everything.

Now think about your own life. Is there a stag you're not pursuing because you don't trust that others will cooperate? It might be a project, a relationship, a difficult conversation you're avoiding. If you identify it, the next question is more interesting: what would you need in order to trust? An explicit promise? A concrete signal? A small first step that proves the other's intention? Sometimes the difference between a life of hares and one of stags is simply asking that question out loud.

Life's big prizes require coordination. The question that determines whether you'll get them isn't whether you want the stag. It's whether you can trust that the other wants it too.

11. The Focal Point: Coordinating Without Words

You're in a huge shopping mall and suddenly realize you've lost your partner. You check your pockets: your phone is in the car. There's no way to call or text. The place has three floors, dozens of stores, multiple entrances. You could spend hours searching without crossing paths. You have to pick a spot and hope your partner picks the same one.

Where do you go?

Most people answer in surprisingly similar ways. Some go to the main entrance. Others to the car. A few to the last store they were in together. Almost nobody picks the fountain on the second floor, the shoe store in the north wing, or the bathroom by the escalator. Without talking, without coordinating, without any prior agreement, people gravitate toward the same places.

This phenomenon has a name: focal point. It's also known as a Schelling point, after the economist who studied it systematically. A focal point is the solution that seems obvious to everyone even though nobody explicitly discussed it. It's the answer that "jumps out" when you need to coordinate with someone without being able to communicate.

A researcher conducted a famous experiment. He asked people: if you had to meet a stranger tomorrow in a large city, with no ability to communicate beforehand, where and when would you go? The responses showed remarkable convergence. Most chose the city's best-known train station, at noon. Not because it was objectively the best place or time, but because it was the most prominent—what any reasonable person would assume another reasonable person would choose.

The focal point works because everyone is looking for the same thing: the option the other person will probably also consider obvious. You don't need to know the other person. You just need to identify what stands out culturally, what's prominent, what has that quality of "this is what anyone would do."

Consider a different situation. Two people must divide a sum of money without communicating. Each writes on paper what percentage they want. If the two percentages add up to one hundred or less, each receives what they asked for. If they add up to more than one hundred, both get nothing. Pure logic says you could ask for any amount. But in practice, the vast majority write fifty. Half and half. Not because it's the only correct answer, but because it's the focal point of "fairness" that both parties recognize without needing to discuss it.

Focal points appear in negotiations, in conflicts, in any situation where coordination matters but communication is limited or impossible. They function as a shared language that doesn't need words.

This has immediate practical applications.

When you find yourself in a situation where you need to coordinate without clear communication, look for the most obvious option. Resist the temptation to be creative or to choose something that makes sense to you but that the other person wouldn't anticipate.

Individual creativity is the enemy of coordination. What you need is to predict what the other person will think, and the best prediction is to assume they're also looking for the obvious.

And when you want others to find you, whether people or opportunities, be predictable. Being where anyone would expect you to be increases the odds of connection. Originality has its place, but in coordination problems, obviousness wins.

The concept extends beyond physical encounters. In a conflict where parties don't speak directly, sometimes a solution emerges that both tacitly accept because it's the natural focal point. In a stalled negotiation, proposing a division that "sounds fair" can break the impasse precisely because both parties recognize it as the point they would gravitate toward if they couldn't negotiate. In tense relationships where communication has broken down, sometimes the first step toward reconciliation is going to the emotional place where the other person is probably also willing to go.

Think now about some conflict or coordination situation in your life where communication is difficult or blocked. If you had to choose a solution that the other party could also choose without talking to you, what would it be? What option is obvious enough that you both would recognize it as the natural meeting point? Identifying that focal point can be the first step to resolving something that seemed like a dead end.

When you can't coordinate explicitly, look for what anyone would do. The obvious solution is your best bet.

12. Repeated Games

You buy fruit from a street vendor in a city you're visiting. The vendor knows he'll probably never see you again. You know it too. If he overcharges you, if the fruit is rotten beneath the visible layer, if the scale is miscalibrated, there are no consequences for him. By the time you realize it, you'll be miles away.

Now think about the baker in your neighborhood, the one you've gone to every week for years. He knows you, you know him. If one day he sells you stale bread or charges you wrong, tomorrow you can come back and complain. Or simply not return. And he knows you can do that. So he doesn't sell you stale bread or charge you wrong. Not because he's more honest than the street vendor, but because his business depends on you coming back.

The difference between these two situations is one of the most powerful forces shaping human behavior: repetition.

A game played once has very different rules from one played indefinitely. When the interaction is one-time, the calculation is simple:

maximize what you can get now, because there won't be a tomorrow with this person. But when you know you'll encounter someone again, the future casts a shadow over the present. The consequences of your actions today extend forward. Betraying now might mean retaliation tomorrow. Cooperating now can build a relationship that pays dividends for years.

This is why you don't cheat your butcher, your mechanic, your work colleagues. The benefit of a scam today is small compared to the cost of losing a relationship that serves you repeatedly. The math changes when the game repeats.

Researchers who studied this phenomenon organized computer tournaments where programs competed in repeated versions of the prisoner's dilemma. Each program had a different strategy: some always cooperated, some always betrayed, some had complex rules based on historical patterns. The winner was one of the simplest. It was called Tit for Tat: start by cooperating, then do exactly what the other did the previous time. If they cooperated, you cooperate. If they betrayed, you betray. Nothing more.

The strategy won because it combined three valuable qualities. It was nice: it never betrayed first. It was vengeful: it immediately punished any betrayal. And it was forgiving: if the other returned to cooperation, it also returned to cooperation without holding an eternal grudge. Simple, clear, predictable. And surprisingly effective against much more sophisticated strategies.

But there's a dangerous moment in repeated games: the end.

When someone knows it's the last interaction, the incentives start to resemble the one-time game again. The vendor closing his shop next week has less reason to care about his reputation. The employee who's already mentally quit has less reason to try hard. The couple who knows the relationship is ending has less reason to invest in it. The end of the game removes the shadow of the future, and without that shadow, the temptation to defect grows.

That's why it's so important to watch for signals that someone perceives the interaction as final. A supplier who starts delivering late might be considering abandoning the relationship. A friend who stops responding to messages might be preparing an exit. It doesn't always mean they'll act badly, but it does mean the mechanism that normally disciplines behavior is weakening.

The most valuable practical application of this concept is actively seeking to convert one-time games into repeated ones. If you can transform an anonymous transaction into a relationship with a name and face, you change everyone's incentives. Return to the same restaurant and the waiter will recognize you. Work with the same supplier and they'll have reasons to take care of you. Build a reputation in your industry and strangers will treat you well because they know others are watching.

Reputation is the mechanism that extends the shadow of the future even to people you'll never see again. If someone knows their behavior toward you will affect how others treat them later, they act as if it were a repeated game even though for you it's one-time. Online reviews work this way. Small professional circles work this way. Communities where "everyone knows everyone" work this way.

Take a moment to think about three relationships in your life that are clearly repeated games. Your partner, perhaps. A colleague you work with constantly. A service provider you use regularly. Now ask yourself: how does your behavior change in these relationships knowing there will be a tomorrow? Are you more patient? More willing to yield in small battles? More careful with your word? The answer reveals how the shadow of the future is already shaping your conduct.

The future disciplines the present. When you know they'll see you tomorrow, you behave better today.

13. Information, Signals, and Commitments: The Power of What's Credible

"I'll pay you, trust me."

"Here's fifty percent up front."

Both sentences promise the same thing. Only one convinces you.

The difference is cost. The first sentence costs nothing to say. Anyone can say it, including those who have no intention of following through. The second sentence costs real money. Only someone who genuinely plans to pay would be willing to hand over cash in advance. The deposit isn't just a partial payment; it's a demonstration of seriousness that words can't match.

This difference between what's said and what's demonstrated runs through almost every interaction where trust matters. And to navigate it well, you need to understand three connected ideas.

The first is that information is almost never distributed equally. In most transactions, one party knows more than the other. The seller of a used car knows every strange noise, every postponed repair, every problem hidden under fresh paint. The buyer only sees what's visible. This asymmetry creates a serious problem: sellers of good cars can't easily distinguish themselves from sellers of bad cars. Everyone says their car is in excellent condition. Words cost nothing.

The result is that buyers, knowing they can't trust words, assume the worst and offer low prices. Sellers of genuinely good cars get frustrated because they can't get what their car is worth. Some decide not to sell. The market fills with problem cars precisely because the good ones withdraw. Distrust becomes a self-fulfilling prophecy.

The second idea is signaling: the way to break this cycle. An effective signal is an action that's easy for someone telling the truth but costly or impossible for someone lying. The seller of a good car can offer an extended warranty covering repairs for six months. If the car has hidden problems, that warranty will cost him a fortune. If the car is fine, it will cost him nothing. Offering the warranty is a credible signal of quality precisely because it would be ruinous to do so with a defective car.

Signals are everywhere once you learn to see them. Four years of university study signal discipline and capacity for sustained effort; getting the degree is hard, which is why it means something. An expensive engagement ring signals seriousness about the relationship; someone planning to leave soon wouldn't make that investment. Arriving early to an interview signals that the position matters to you; if it didn't matter, you wouldn't sacrifice your time. What makes these signals credible is exactly what makes them hard to fake: they cost something real.

The third idea takes this a step further: the credible commitment. Sometimes the most powerful way to signal your intentions is to eliminate your own options to back out.

There's a famous story of a conquistador who, upon arriving in enemy territory, ordered his own ships burned. His soldiers, watching the only escape route go up in flames, understood that the only way out was forward. But the most important message wasn't for them; it was for the enemy. Now the defenders knew they faced an army with no possibility of retreat, an army that would fight to the end because it had no alternative. The conquistador became more dangerous precisely because he removed his own options.

The principle appears in less dramatic contexts. A non-refundable deposit commits you to show up. A public announcement of your goals commits you to pursue them because now your reputation is at stake. Giving your word to someone specific, face to face, commits you more than a vague promise because the social cost of failure increases.

In negotiations, this principle can give you paradoxical power. "My boss authorized me up to this figure, I can't move from there" eliminates your flexibility. But that elimination makes you more credible. The other party knows you're not playing, that you genuinely can't yield more, and that can make them yield first. Your apparent weakness becomes real strength.

The pattern is consistent: words are cheap, costly actions are credible, and sometimes the best way to commit yourself is to remove the possibility of not following through.

Now think about some promise you need to make credible in your life. It might be a commitment to another person or to yourself. Ask yourself what costly signal you could send to demonstrate you're serious. Is there something you could do that would be easy if your intention is genuine but difficult if you're lying? Is there some way to eliminate your option to back out, to burn your own boats, so that both you and others know there's no turning back?

Words convince, but costly actions prove. Sometimes, limiting your options gives you more power.

14. The Game of Chicken, or Who Blinks First

Two cars accelerate toward each other in opposite directions on the same lane. The first to swerve loses: they're "chicken," a coward, the one who couldn't take it. The one who holds course wins prestige, respect, the admiration of onlookers. But if neither swerves, both die. The simplest game to explain and the most dangerous to play.

What makes this game different from everything we've seen so far is the nature of the worst possible outcome. In the prisoner's dilemma we explored earlier, betraying when the other cooperated gave you the best individual gain. Here it doesn't work that way. Holding firm when the other also holds firm doesn't give you victory. It gives you destruction. The crash has no winner.

Yielding is bad. You feel humiliated, defeated, the one who blinked first. But yielding is survivable. You can go home, lick your wounds, live to fight another day. Not yielding when the other doesn't yield either is something else entirely. It's the end of the game with no possibility of a rematch.

This asymmetry between "bad" and "catastrophic" appears disguised in situations you face regularly.

You're negotiating your salary with a potential employer. You want one figure, they offer a lower one. Each negotiation round is one step closer to the center of the lane. If you yield first, you accept less than you wanted. It hurts, but you have the job. If they yield first, you get what you asked for. But if nobody yields, there's no deal. You leave without a job, they're left without a candidate. Both lose more than they would have lost by yielding.

A labor strike works the same way. Workers want better conditions, the company wants to control costs. Each day of the strike is a day without production for the company and a day without wages for the workers. If the company yields first, the workers win. If the workers yield first, they return with less than they asked for. But if nobody yields and the strike extends indefinitely, the company can go bankrupt and the workers are left with nowhere to return. The crash destroys both.

In couple relationships, the game of chicken appears whenever there's a conflict where neither wants to be the first to apologize. Both know someone has to yield for the relationship to continue. Both feel that yielding first means admitting guilt, losing the argument, ending up in a weak position. Days pass in tense silence. Each waits for the other to break first. And sometimes nobody does, and what was a repairable fight becomes a permanent crack.

There's a strategy that seems brilliant in this game: convince the other that you won't yield no matter what. If your opponent genuinely believes you're willing to go all the way to the crash, the rational decision for them is to swerve. After all, better to be chicken than dead.

This is the strategy of "looking crazy." Projecting an image of calculated irrationality. "I don't care about the consequences, I'm not moving, do what you want." The negotiator who says "this is my final offer, take it or leave it" and seems to mean it has an advantage. The spouse who seems genuinely willing to destroy the relationship rather than apologize first puts pressure on the other to yield.

The problem is obvious: if both try to look crazy, both crash. The strategy only works if only one uses it. And there's no way to know beforehand if the other is also using it.

There's a better way out than simply waiting to see who blinks first or who projects more convincing madness.

The way out is to offer the other person a way to yield that doesn't feel like defeat.

Think about what the other person needs to be able to move. Almost always, what prevents yielding isn't the material cost but the cost to pride. Nobody wants to look like the weak one, the one who lost, the one who couldn't take it. But if you can reframe the situation so that yielding seems like gaining something different, you change the equation.

In salary negotiation: "I understand you can't reach the figure I asked for. What if we accept a lower number but with a guaranteed review in six months?" The employer didn't yield on salary, they gained time and commitment. You didn't completely yield, you secured a review. Both can declare victory.

In the strike: "We return to work at current salary, but with a joint committee to review conditions in ninety days." The workers didn't lose, they gained a formal voice. The company didn't lose, it recovered immediate production. The crash was avoided because nobody had to admit defeat.

In the couple's fight: "We both probably said things we didn't mean. Should we start over?" Nobody had to apologize first. Nobody had to admit exclusive guilt. Both can emerge from the silence without humiliating themselves.

The key is understanding that the person in front of you probably doesn't want the crash any more than you do. What they want is not to lose face. If you give them a way to move that preserves their dignity, most of the time they'll take it.

This requires a shift in mindset. Instead of thinking "how do I make the other person yield?", the more useful question is "how do I make yielding not feel like losing?"

Examine the active conflicts in your life right now. Is there one where both parties are waiting for the other to yield first? If there is, instead of holding firm waiting for the other to blink, consider what dignified exit you could offer them. What could they gain by moving that would make the move less humiliating? Sometimes the answer is as simple as changing the language: instead of "you were right and I was wrong," something like "let's find a solution that works for both of us."

In conflicts where someone must yield first, the winner is rarely the one who shouts loudest or seems most willing to engage in mutual destruction. The winner is the one who understands that their opponent also wants to avoid the crash and offers them a way to do so without losing face. Building those dignified exits is harder than simply holding firm, but it's infinitely more effective than waiting to see who destroys themselves first.

15. Who Defines the Game: First Mover Advantage and Anchoring

Fifty thousand. That's what you said when they asked how much you wanted to earn. You didn't think too hard about it. It was a round number, reasonable, maybe a bit above what you had before. The interviewer nodded, took notes, and the conversation moved on. Half an hour later, when it came time to talk compensation, the offer was forty-seven thousand. You negotiated a bit, landed at forty-eight five, and closed the deal. You left satisfied.

What you never knew is that the approved budget for that position went up to sixty-five thousand.

The number you tossed out in the first minutes of the conversation became the center of gravity for the entire negotiation. Everything that came after—the counteroffers, the adjustments, the "maximum effort" that HR supposedly made—revolved around your initial figure. Not around the actual value of the position, not around the range the company had in mind, not around what other candidates with your experience were asking for. Around what you said first.

You just experienced the power of the anchor.

In any negotiation where numbers are discussed—salary, sale price, contract terms, division of responsibilities—the first value put on the table exerts a disproportionate influence on the final outcome. Researchers have documented this effect repeatedly: when two groups are asked to estimate the value of something, but each group is given a different initial number as a "starting point," the final estimates from both groups gravitate toward their respective starting points, even when those initial numbers were completely arbitrary.

The anchor works because the human brain needs a reference point to evaluate proposals. When someone says "eighty thousand," your mind automatically starts calculating distances from that number. Seventy-five thousand feels like a significant concession. Sixty thousand seems like an aggressive offer. But if the first number had been "sixty thousand," then fifty-five thousand would feel like the significant concession, and forty-five thousand like the aggressive offer. The same absolute numbers are perceived radically differently depending on where the conversation started.

This means whoever speaks first has a structural advantage: they define the territory where the entire battle will take place. The other participants, even if they don't notice it, will be reacting to that first move instead of operating from their own parameters.

But here comes the complication: moving first is only an advantage when you know what you're doing.

If you know the range of reasonable values for what you're negotiating well—because you researched the market, because you have experience in similar transactions, because you did your homework—anchoring first allows you to establish the most favorable starting point for yourself. You ask for more than you expect to get, knowing that negotiation will move you down, but from an elevated position. Or if you're buying, you offer less than you're willing to pay, knowing they'll move you up, but from a low floor.

The key is that your anchor must be ambitious but not absurd. A number too far from reality doesn't anchor the conversation; it destroys it. If the position pays in the range of sixty to eighty thousand and you ask for two hundred thousand, you haven't anchored anything. You've demonstrated that you don't understand the market, or that you're not negotiating seriously. The other side will discard your number completely and the conversation will restart on their terms, not yours.

But there are situations where speaking first is a mistake.

When you have no idea of the other side's range—when you genuinely don't know how much they're willing to pay, or how much they expect to receive—letting them anchor first gives you valuable information. Their initial number reveals their frame of reference, their expectations, perhaps even their limitations. Sometimes you discover they were willing to offer more than you would have asked for. Other times you confirm they're well below your acceptable minimum, and you can walk away without having shown your cards.

The question before each negotiation, then, is twofold: how much do I know about the real range of this transaction? And based on that, should I anchor or let them anchor?

Now suppose you didn't move first. The other side threw out their number, and it's much worse than you expected. Your instinct is to react from there: "That's very low, could you go up to...?" Wrong. The moment you start negotiating from their number, you've accepted their anchor. Your counteroffer, however aggressive, will still orbit around the planet they placed at the center of the solar system.

The effective defense against an adverse anchor is to ignore it completely. Don't discuss it, don't analyze it, don't explain why it's inadequate. Simply present your own anchor as if theirs never existed. "That's very far from what I had in mind. I was thinking something closer to..." and you release your number. Now there are two anchors competing for the center of gravity, and negotiation can begin from more balanced ground.

This requires preparation. You can't improvise your own anchor the moment they hit you with an unexpected one. The surprise of a low or high number can paralyze you, make you doubt, lead you to accept their frame before your mind reacts. That's why the work starts before the conversation. You decide in advance what number you're going to put on the table if it's your turn to anchor, and also what number you'll use as a counter-anchor if they go first. You arrive at the negotiation with both figures clear in your head, ready to deploy depending on how the opening unfolds.

In your next opportunity—whether it's a salary negotiation, buying a used item, hiring a service, any situation where numbers are in play—prepare your anchor before you enter. Write it down if you need to. And when the moment comes, practice it: don't release it as a question, don't present it with apologies, don't soften it with "I don't know if this is reasonable but..." Say it with the same naturalness you'd say your name.

The first number in a negotiation isn't just an initial proposal. It's the center of gravity around which everything else will move. Whoever puts down that number defines the playing field. And once you understand this, you have an advantage that most people don't even know exists.

16. Positions and Interests

Two sisters fight over an orange. Each insists she needs it. The argument escalates, their mother intervenes, and the Solomonic solution seems obvious: cut the fruit in half. Perfect justice. Except one sister throws her half in the trash after grating the peel for a cake, while the other squeezes her half and discards the rest. Between the two of them, they had one whole orange. They ended up with half each. The "fair" division gave both of them exactly half of what they could have gotten.

The problem wasn't lack of generosity or ill will. The problem was that both said "I want the orange" when they actually wanted completely different things. One needed the peel, the other the juice. Their needs were perfectly compatible. But because they negotiated over what they were asking for instead of why they were asking for it, neither got what they really wanted.

This distinction between what you declare and what you need runs through practically every negotiation you'll face in your life. What you say you want is your position: the specific job, the exact price, the particular schedule, the concrete division of tasks. Why you want it is your interest: the underlying need that position is trying to satisfy. Positions are rigid and often incompatible. Interests are flexible and frequently can be satisfied in multiple ways.

When two people clash over opposing positions, it seems like only one can win. You want the car for thirty thousand, the seller offers it for forty thousand. You want to work from home, your boss wants you in the office. You want a beach vacation, your partner wants mountains. In each case, the stated positions are mutually exclusive. The game appears to be zero-sum: what one gains, the other loses.

But it's rarely like that once you look beneath the surface.

The car seller perhaps doesn't need forty thousand specifically; he needs to cover what he owes on the vehicle and have something for the down payment on the next one. If his debt is thirty-two thousand, there's room for an agreement that seemed impossible minutes ago.

Your boss perhaps doesn't need your physical presence in the office; she needs to know you'll be available for urgent meetings and that the team will maintain cohesion. If you offer to be present two critical days per week and available by video call anytime, her real interest is covered even though your original position isn't met literally.

The technique for uncovering hidden interests is almost embarrassingly simple: ask why. And keep asking.

Someone says they want a raise. First layer: they want more money. But why do they want more money? To feel valued. Why do they need to feel valued? Because they've been working harder than anyone for a year and nobody has acknowledged it. Suddenly, the conversation has completely changed. What seemed like a negotiation about numbers reveals itself as a need for recognition. And recognition can be given in many ways: a new title, a public mention, a visible project, expanded responsibilities. Maybe the raise comes too, but now you know it's not the only thing that would solve the problem. Maybe it's not even the main thing.

This chain of "whys" usually needs between three and five iterations before reaching the true interest. The first answer is almost always superficial, a restatement of the original position. The second starts to reveal motivations. By the third or fourth, something more fundamental usually emerges: security, respect, autonomy, connection, sense of purpose. These deep interests are what really move people, and they're much more malleable than the concrete positions they express.

Let's return to the vacation conflict. One person's position is beach, the other's is mountains. The typical compromise would be to alternate years or find a middle ground that excites nobody. But if you explore the interests, you discover that the person asking for beach is seeking rest: days without agenda, sun, long reads. The person asking for mountains is seeking adventure: movement, new landscapes, the feeling of having done something. Those interests aren't contradictory. There are places with coastline and trails. There are itineraries where mornings are for exploring and afternoons for resting by the water. There are destinations where both interests are completely satisfied, but that neither would have proposed while the discussion revolved around "beach versus mountains."

Now, for this technique to work, someone has to take the first step and reveal their real interest. There's vulnerability there. Saying "I want the beach" is safe; saying "I need to rest because I'm exhausted and feel like my life is slipping away" exposes something deeper. But that exposure is precisely what opens doors. When you share your true why, you invite the other to do the same. And once both interests are on the table, creativity can flow toward solutions that rigid positions blocked.

In your next discussion where you feel positions are stuck, before defending your position with more arguments, try something different. Ask the other person: "What's most important to you in this?" And after hearing their answer, ask "Why does that matter so much to you?" Not as a challenge or as an interrogation technique. As genuine curiosity. The answer you get will probably change your understanding of the entire conflict.

The sisters with the orange could have ended up each with exactly what she needed. One with all the peel, the other with all the juice. Zero waste, zero sacrifice. The only thing they lacked was one question: not what do you want, but why do you want it. That question changes everything.

17. Escalation and De-escalation: Getting Out of the Anger Game

It started with a comment about the dirty dishes. An observation, almost innocent, about how they'd been piling up by the sink for three days. The response was a bit sharper: something about who works more hours and who has more time. The reply raised the tone. References appeared to other occasions, to patterns, to that time last month. Suddenly they weren't talking about dishes anymore but about respect, about priorities, about whether they really cared about each other. Twenty minutes later, both were in furious silence in separate rooms. Neither remembered clearly how they'd gotten there. What they both knew was that they weren't going to be the one to give in first.

This pattern has a precise mechanics. Each move in an escalation follows logic that seems perfectly reasonable in the moment: if the other person raised the intensity, I can't fall behind. Responding with less force would feel like losing ground, like admitting guilt, like letting the other person "win." So you match or go up a bit more. The other person feels exactly the same, so they also match or raise. And the cycle continues, each round a bit more intense than the last, until the damage caused far exceeds what was originally at stake.

What's fascinating is that at every moment of escalation, backing down seems like the worst option. The cost of taking a step back—the feeling of defeat, the humiliation of being the one who blinks first—feels immense. Meanwhile, the cost of continuing seems smaller: just one more comment, just one more response, just holding your position a little longer. The problem is that perception is distorted. Pride magnifies the price of backing down and minimizes the price of continuing. That's why so many people end up preferring to lose a hundred fighting rather than win eighty by yielding.

But the real costs of escalating don't appear in the heat of the moment. They appear afterward. The emotional energy you consumed that you no longer have for other things. The time that went into a battle that improved nothing. And above all, the damage to the relationship: the words you said in the intensity of the conflict that you can't take back, the trust that eroded, the distance that settled between you. Sometimes "winning" a fight leaves you in a worse position than having lost it. You kept your pride intact but damaged something worth more.

Getting out of this game requires someone to break the pattern. And breaking the pattern feels, in the moment, like surrendering. That's the psychological trap. But there are ways to interrupt the escalation without handing victory to the other person.

The simplest is the physical pause. Say "I need ten minutes" and remove yourself from the space. Not as a strategy to gain advantage or as silent punishment. As genuine recognition that your nervous system is too activated to think clearly. The pause gives your brain time to exit combat mode and remember what really matters to you. What seemed like a life-or-death matter a minute ago, after a short walk or a glass of water, usually reveals itself as something manageable.

Another technique is to reframe what's happening. In the middle of the fight, both of you are acting as if you're enemies. But you probably aren't. Probably, beneath the conflict, you both want to solve something. Saying it out loud changes the dynamic: "We both want to fix this, right?" That simple phrase reminds you that you're on the same side even though you disagree. The enemy isn't the other person; the enemy is the problem you're trying to solve.

A third tool is to offer concrete options instead of abstract positions. When the discussion becomes about who's right and who's wrong, there's no exit that doesn't feel like defeat for someone. But when the conversation moves to "Would you prefer we do A or we do B?", a path appears. Concrete options give something specific to decide on, instead of a nebulous territory of pride and principles where nobody can yield without feeling humiliated.

These techniques can be combined into something like a script that works in a surprising number of situations. Start by acknowledging what the other person feels: "I see you're frustrated." That alone, without arguing whether they're right to be, lowers the temperature. Then remind them of the shared interest: "I also want us to solve this." Finally, offer alternatives: "What if we do this, or try that?" The complete pattern takes less than thirty seconds and defuses most escalations before they reach the point of no return.

The next time you feel a discussion rising in intensity—voices getting louder, arguments turning to the past, words starting to cut—try something. Stop. Breathe. And say: "Wait. What do we really want to accomplish here?" Not as a rhetorical trick but as a genuine question. Watch what happens when you both have to pause the combat to think about the answer. Sometimes that's enough for the anger game to lose its momentum.

There's a mistaken perception that whoever stops an escalation is the one who lost. As if stopping first were admitting defeat. The reality is exactly the opposite. In an escalation, the first to stop isn't the loser. They're the only adult in the room.

18. When You Can't Win, Change the Rules

A small coffee shop opens on a corner where there are already three major chain locations within a few blocks. The numbers are brutal: the chains buy beans by the ton, negotiate prices the small place will never get, and can offer promotions that would eat through any profit margin the smaller competitor might have. If the game is who sells the cheapest coffee, the outcome is decided before it starts.

But the small coffee shop doesn't play that game. It plays a completely different one. The barista learns regular customers' names, remembers their orders, asks how last week's interview went. The space is quieter, more personal, without the rushed line of people who just want their cup and to leave. The coffee might cost a bit more. But there are customers willing to pay that difference for something no chain can easily replicate: feeling that someone recognizes them, that the place is theirs.

Same industry. Same basic product. Victory in a game the big players don't even know they're playing.

This logic applies far beyond business. Every time you find yourself in a situation where the rules of the game seem to guarantee your defeat, you have more options than it appears. You can keep playing the game that favors the other side and lose predictably. Or you can ask yourself what would need to change for the terrain to tilt toward you.

The first possibility is to change the rules of competition itself. When everyone competes on price, you compete on speed. When everyone competes on speed, you compete on quality. When everyone competes on quality, you compete on experience, on customization, on something your particular strengths allow you to offer that others ignore or can't replicate. The professional who can't charge the highest rates in the market might be able to differentiate by being the easiest to work with, the most flexible with deadlines, the one who responds in minutes instead of days. The job candidate who doesn't have the most impressive resume might be the one who listens best, who asks the smartest questions, who demonstrates hunger to learn. Changing the rules means identifying a dimension of competition that favors you and making that dimension the one that matters.

The second possibility is to change who the players are. Sometimes your enemy's enemy is your natural ally. Competitors who would individually lose to a larger player can form alliances to create a common front: share resources, divide markets, collaborate where it benefits them and compete only where necessary. In other cases, changing the players means eliminating intermediaries who capture value without contributing it, or introducing new participants whose presence alters the dynamics. A negotiation where you're alone facing a powerful counterpart can transform if you bring in a third party—an expert, a witness, an ally—whose presence modifies everyone's behavior.

The third possibility is to change the success criteria. If you can't win on the metric everyone assumes is relevant, the question is whether that metric is really what matters to you. In a salary negotiation where the maximum number they're offering is below what you wanted, the game of "getting more money" is lost. But the game of "getting better conditions" might be completely open: additional vacation days, flexible hours, remote work possibility, access to interesting projects, a different title. None of those things appear in the salary number, but they all affect your quality of life. Redefining what counts as victory lets you win battles you didn't even know you were fighting.

This has very personal applications.

Think about an argument with your partner where you're both defending incompatible positions. The apparent game is "winning the argument": proving your point of view is correct, that the other should yield, that you're right. But if you win that game, what do you lose? You probably lose connection. The other person probably feels unheard, defeated, resentful. You won the battle and weakened the relationship. The problem wasn't your argument. The problem was the game you chose to play. The right game perhaps wasn't "winning the argument" but "understanding each other better" or "finding something that works for both of us" or even "showing them I care more about the relationship than being right." In that different game, the winning moves are completely different.

There's a natural resistance to changing games. Part of us wants to prove we can win on the original terrain, even when that terrain is designed for our defeat. Pride ties us to battles we shouldn't be fighting. But the truth is you don't get points for persisting in games you can't win. You get them for achieving what matters to you.

Think now about some competition where you feel you're at a disadvantage. It could be at work, in a relationship, in any area where the rules seem to favor others. Instead of asking yourself how to win that game, ask something different: what different game could you create where your particular strengths—the things you do better than most, the unique resources you have, the advantages others ignore—are what determine the outcome?

Conventional wisdom says you have to play to win. But strategic wisdom says something different: first make sure you're playing the right game. Don't fight battles designed for you to lose. Change the battlefield.

19. Game Theory in Relationships

"Why do I always have to be the one to wash the dishes?"

That sentence, spoken with frustration after dinner, hides more than it seems. Behind it is a prisoner's dilemma that neither recognizes. There's asymmetric information: each believes they do more than the other, and both are right from their perspective. There's a poorly designed negotiation that was never made explicit. And there's a silent game of chicken where neither wants to yield first because doing so feels like losing.

Living together as a couple is the most important repeated game you'll play in your life. Two interdependent people, making decisions that affect both, for years or decades. Each small interaction accumulates. Each pattern reinforces itself. And unlike almost any other relationship, there's no boss to arbitrate, no formal contract to consult, no neutral third party to say who's right. Just the two of you, implicitly negotiating thousands of small agreements every week.

What's extraordinary is that most of those negotiations are never verbalized.

Let's return to the dishes. If both expect the other to wash them, nobody washes them. The kitchen fills with dirty dishes, resentment grows, and eventually someone explodes. The classic prisoner's dilemma pattern: each acting according to their individual convenience produces a result both hate. The difference from the original dilemma is that here there are no separate interrogation rooms. You live together. You can talk. You can design a better system.

Solutions work when they're made explicit. Clear turns eliminate ambiguity: you wash today, I wash tomorrow. Specialization leverages differences: maybe one hates washing but doesn't mind cooking, while the other prefers the reverse. Each does what they detest least. Outsourcing recognizes that sometimes the conflict costs more than avoiding it: hiring household help might be cheaper than recurring fights.

But there's a deeper problem that no rotation system solves: asymmetric perception of effort.

Both genuinely feel they do more. And both are right from their point of view. You remember perfectly every time you washed dishes, took out the trash, scheduled a doctor's appointment. But those tasks the other did while you weren't looking—the bank call, buying what was missing, the message to the relative who needed contacting—those register less. The result is a mental ledger where each sees themselves contributing sixty or seventy percent. The math doesn't add up, but both accounts are emotionally true.

The solution requires bringing what remains invisible into the light. An exercise that works surprisingly well: sit down with your partner and do a joint inventory. Each lists everything they believe they contribute to shared life—not just household tasks, but also emotional labor, family logistics, maintaining social relationships, financial planning. Then exchange lists. The goal is for each person to add to the other's list the things they'd forgotten or hadn't noticed. What almost always happens is that both lists grow significantly. Not because someone was lying, but because it's impossible to see everything the other does when you're not watching.

From that inventory something more formal can emerge: an expectations contract. It sounds unromantic, but couples that work have these agreements even though they rarely call them that. What "helping" means in this house. How to ask for help without it sounding like reproach. How to signal when something isn't working without it escalating to a fight. Three clear points, agreed on in a moment of calm, can prevent dozens of future conflicts.

And then there are the fights. Those arguments where both entrench themselves in opposing positions and neither wants to be the first to yield.

The chapter on the game of chicken described this dynamic in negotiation contexts. In couples, it appears with disturbing frequency. An argument ends without resolution. Both go to sleep upset. Days pass and neither mentions the topic because doing so feels like admitting guilt. The silence thickens. Each waits for the other to take the first step. And since neither does, the original conflict—which was perhaps minor—transforms into something larger: an unresolved grievance that contaminates future interactions.

The way out is to offer what we earlier called "dignified exits." A move that allows both to back down without anyone losing. Instead of "you were right and I was wrong"—a phrase almost nobody says voluntarily—something like "we were both frustrated, should we start over?" changes the dynamic. There's no winner or loser. There are two people who recognize the conflict cost them both and prefer to leave it behind.

This requires abandoning the zero-sum mentality that infects so many couple arguments. When the implicit question is "who's right?", only one can win. But when the question transforms into "how can we both get what we need?", options appear that the previous question hid.

The vacation example—one wants beach, the other wants mountains—illustrates this clearly. Fighting over the destination assumes the pie is fixed. Exploring the interests beneath the positions might reveal that one seeks rest and the other seeks adventure, and that destinations exist where both find what they need. The fight was unnecessary. What was missing was the right question.

The temptation in any romantic relationship is to treat each disagreement as a battle to win. But the time horizon changes everything. You're going to wake up next to this person tomorrow, and next week, and possibly twenty years from now. Each pyrrhic victory—that argument you "won" but that left resentment—accumulates. Today's small victories become long-term defeats.

The real game was never winning tonight's argument. The real game is continuing to build something together for decades. And in that game, winning the argument and losing the relationship isn't winning anything.

20. Parents and Children: Incentives and Tantrums

"If you don't eat your vegetables, no dessert."

The child looks at the plate. Stabs a piece of broccoli with the fork. Brings it close to his mouth. Pulls it away. Finally, he eats two microscopic bites and announces he's done. Now he wants dessert.

You have a fraction of a second to decide. On one hand, technically he ate some vegetables. On the other, you both know that wasn't what you meant. If you give him dessert, you've taught him that rules are negotiable and that resistance works. If you don't give it to him, tears will come, possibly a tantrum, and the peaceful dinner you imagined will become a battlefield.

But the real question is different: how many times have you been here before? And on those previous occasions, what did you do?

If the honest answer is that sometimes you gave in, the game was already lost before sitting down at the table tonight. The child learned, through systematic experimentation, that your threats have a success rate of less than one hundred percent. And like any rational player, he keeps betting on that margin.

Parenting is a repeated game where credibility determines almost everything.

Children arrive in the world without an instruction manual for how it works. They spend their first years conducting continuous experiments: if I do this, what happens? If I cry louder, does the outcome change? If I insist ten times, is the answer still no? Each interaction delivers data. And they process that data with an efficiency that would embarrass any scientist.

When you say "if you don't do X, then Y" and then don't apply Y, the child doesn't register that you had a bad day or that you were tired or that just this once you made an exception. He registers that threats don't always come true. And that information is pure gold for someone mapping the limits of his universe. Next time, he'll resist a little more. He'll test whether today is also an exception day.

Consistency today prevents tantrums tomorrow. It sounds cruel in the moment—maintaining a consequence when the crying intensifies and everyone in the restaurant is staring at you—but it's a long-term investment. The child who learns early that rules are solid stops testing them. The one who learns they're flexible never stops pushing.

This leads to the tantrum, which deserves its own analysis.

A tantrum looks like an emotional collapse, and partly it is. But it's also a strategic move, frequently executed with calibrated precision. The child has learned that the tantrum has costs for you: public embarrassment, exhaustion, the desperate desire for the noise to stop. The implicit bet is clear: I'm going to cause you enough trouble until the cost of maintaining your position exceeds the cost of giving in.

If you give in once, the bet paid off. And like any successful strategy, it will repeat. The next tantrum will be a bit longer, a bit more intense, because the child learned that resistance has a breaking point and that it's worth seeking it.

The way out isn't to get tougher or yell louder. It's to make the bet stop being profitable. When the tantrum never produces the desired result—never, without exceptions, regardless of duration or intensity—it stops making sense as a strategy. Children aren't masochists; they abandon tactics that don't work. But they need enough data to reach that conclusion.

Designing incentives that work requires attention to three principles.

The first is immediacy. A consequence that will arrive "when we get home" loses force with each passing minute. The child's brain connects cause and effect more easily when they're close in time. "You didn't share the toy, so now I'm putting it away for five minutes" teaches more than "because of this you won't have dessert after dinner."

The second is proportionality. Disproportionate threats—"if you don't clean your room, no TV for a month"—have a fatal problem: you're not going to enforce them. The child knows it. You know it. A consequence you'll actually apply, even if minor, has more power than a dramatic threat both of you know is theater.

The third is consistency. The same action should produce the same consequence, regardless of your mood, the day of the week, or whether you have an audience. Rules that change according to context aren't rules; they're suggestions the child will learn to negotiate.

Now, this model works differently when children grow up.

The teenager is no longer a child experimenting with the universe's limits. He's someone with his own options, his own information, and a growing need for autonomy. Imposing authority works when you control resources and access. But the teenager can lie about where he is, can get what he wants through friends, can simply stop communicating with you.

The game changed because the other player has more cards.

The smart transition is from imposition to negotiation. Instead of "the rules are these because I say so," something closer to "these are the reasons behind the rules, and I'm willing to adjust them if you demonstrate you can handle more freedom." The teenager who feels he has a voice in decisions has less need to rebel. The one who feels the rules are arbitrary and imposed will seek ways to evade them.

This requires letting go of control—something difficult for someone who's been the final authority for years—but the alternative is worse. Authority imposed on a teenager who no longer accepts it simply becomes constant conflict. Renegotiating rules allows you to maintain real influence in exchange for yielding apparent control.

Think about some rule in your house that's frequently broken. Ask yourself: is the established consequence credible? Do you apply it every time the rule is broken? If the answer to either of these questions is no, you have two options. You can redesign the rule so the consequence is enforceable and proportional. Or you can accept that particular rule isn't that important and stop pretending it is. Both options are better than maintaining a fiction everyone knows is fiction.

What children seek when they test limits isn't to destroy them. It's to know which ones are real. They need a map of the territory, a clear idea of where the edges are. Your job is to show them with enough consistency that they stop asking.

21. Friendships, Reciprocity, and Strategic Forgiveness

Third time they've canceled. The message arrived two hours before the dinner you'd planned weeks ago. Something came up, they say. So sorry. Next time for sure.

Next time. You know that phrase well.

Now you have to decide what to do. You could let it slide, respond with an understanding emoji and carry on as if nothing happened. You could push back, express that this is becoming a pattern and it bothers you. You could simply stop inviting them, quietly pull back and see if they notice your absence. Each option has costs and each sends a different message.

The question you're probably not asking yourself, but which determines the right answer, is different: how many chances does someone deserve before you stop giving them?

Friendships function as sustained cooperation equilibria. Two people who choose, again and again, to invest time and energy in each other. When the investment is reciprocal, the friendship strengthens. When it's one-sided, one person is being exploited. The difficulty lies in distinguishing a bad moment from a bad pattern.

There's a strategy that works remarkably well in repeated cooperation situations. Researchers who organized computer tournaments to test different approaches discovered that one of the simplest was also one of the most effective: start by cooperating, respond to what the other does, but always leave the door open to cooperate again if they change. Be kind initially, proportional in response, willing to forgive if there's genuine correction.

Applied to friendships, this means giving people the benefit of the doubt initially. Everyone has real emergencies, impossible weeks, moments when they simply can't follow through. Punishing the first failure as if it were betrayal destroys relationships that could have been valuable. But that initial generosity must be accompanied by attention to patterns. If cancellations repeat, if promises are never kept, if investment consistently flows in one direction, the information is clear.

Detecting a parasitic friendship requires observing more than feeling. The signals are fairly consistent. You're always the one initiating contact; if you stop texting, the conversation dies. You're always the one proposing plans; if you wait for them to suggest something, you wait indefinitely. When you go out, somehow you end up paying more or covering expenses that are never returned. When you need something—a favor, an ear, a hand—the person is busy, absent, or responds lukewarmly. But when they need something from you, they appear with urgency and expectations.

None of these signals in isolation means much. All of them together, sustained over time, reveal a structure.

The simplest test is to stop initiating and observe what happens. If the friendship survives without your constant momentum, there was reciprocity you weren't seeing. If it vanishes completely the moment you stop rowing, you have your answer. The resulting silence is valuable information, even if it hurts to receive it.

Now, there's an opposite error that also carries high costs: eternal resentment.

Someone failed you. They genuinely disappointed you. The natural reaction is to protect yourself: build a wall, keep your distance, remember the offense every time they try to get close. The problem is this strategy has terrible math. If the person changed—if they acknowledged their mistake, if they adjusted their behavior, if they're making visible efforts—punishing them forever destroys value that both of you could be generating.

Strategic forgiveness recognizes that keeping someone in the "untrustworthy" category has an opportunity cost. That person could have become a valuable ally, someone who learned from their mistake and is now more reliable precisely because they know what's at stake. Eternal resentment assumes people don't change. Sometimes that's true. But sometimes it isn't, and refusing to see evidence of real change is stubbornness disguised as prudence.

The key is distinguishing between giving opportunities and being naive. An opportunity is a test: let's see if the behavior changed. If it changed, the relationship can be rebuilt. If it didn't change, now you have more data to make an informed decision. The naive person ignores the data and keeps expecting different results from the same behaviors.

There's a point where ending a friendship is the right decision. If the pattern is consistently negative after multiple clear opportunities, if the person has repeatedly demonstrated they won't change, withdrawing is rational. The guilt you feel doing it is understandable—no one wants to be the person who abandons a relationship—but remaining in a dynamic that damages you isn't loyalty. It's self-harm.

Withdrawing doesn't require drama either. Sometimes it's enough to stop investing energy and allow natural distance to do its work. The friendship fades not because you explicitly ended it, but because it stopped being fed. It's a quiet death, but often cleaner than confrontation.

There's one curious phenomenon worth mentioning because it contradicts intuition.

Asking for favors can strengthen friendships rather than weaken them. Conventional logic says asking for things is a burden, that you impose when you request help, that you should minimize what you ask to avoid bothering people. But there's a well-documented psychological effect that works in reverse: whoever does you a favor becomes more committed to you, not less.

The reason is that the brain seeks coherence. If I helped you, it must be because I care about you—otherwise, why would I have invested my time and energy? The act of helping creates an internal narrative that reinforces the relationship. Obviously this has limits; constantly asking without reciprocating eventually exhausts anyone. But within those limits, allowing others to help you brings them closer rather than pushing them away.

Think about your current friendships now. In one of them, are you punishing someone who has perhaps already changed, denying them the opportunity to prove it? In another, are you tolerating a pattern that clearly won't improve, waiting for a change that never comes? Both questions deserve honest answers. The first might return a valuable relationship to you. The second might free you from one that isn't.

The formula that works in friendships is the same one that works in other contexts of repeated cooperation: generous at the start, proportional in response, willing to forgive if there's real change. Not so soft that you get exploited, not so hard that you destroy what could have been saved.

22. Family, Inheritances, Coalitions, and Christmas

Grandmother dies on a Tuesday. The wake is Thursday, the burial Friday. By Sunday, three siblings who grew up together, who shared a bedroom for decades, who swore they loved each other unconditionally, have stopped speaking.

The house is the problem. Grandmother left it to all three in equal shares, with no instructions about what to do with it. Two want to sell: they need the money, they live far away, there's no point maintaining a property no one will use. One wants to keep it: he grew up there, there are memories in every wall, the idea of a stranger living where he took his first steps feels unbearable.

Mathematically, the solution exists. The brother who wants the house could buy out the other two. Or they could sell it and split three ways. Or they could rent it out and divide the income. The options are there.

But nobody's doing math. They're processing grief, decades of family dynamics, resentments that were never verbalized, the feeling that this decision will define who really loved grandmother and who just wanted her money. The brother who wants to sell feels accused of being cold and materialistic. The one who wants to keep it feels the others want to erase the family memory for a check. Three months later, two of them aren't speaking. A year later, their children aren't speaking either. A forty-year relationship, destroyed by a house.

This is the game no one chose to play.

You didn't choose your siblings. You didn't choose your uncles, cousins, in-laws. They appeared in your life by accident of birth or through others' romantic decisions. And yet, these people will be present at funerals, weddings, and awkward dinners for the rest of your existence. The time horizon is eternal. The emotional consequences, enormous. And the potential for destruction, absolute.

Inheritances are the most dangerous minefield because they're pure zero-sum.

There's a fixed amount of resources and every dollar one person receives is a dollar the others don't. Worse still: the moment of division coincides exactly with the moment of greatest emotional vulnerability. Someone just died. Everyone is processing loss. And in that state they have to make significant financial decisions while their brains search for signals of who was the favorite, who deserves more, who's taking advantage of the situation.

The only effective solution is prevention. Clear wills that leave no room for interpretation. Advance conversations—uncomfortable, yes, but infinitely less painful than the alternatives—about who wants what and why. Transparent division where everyone understands the logic, even if not everyone is happy with the result. The time to design these rules is when the person is still alive, when there's time to discuss, adjust, and reach agreements everyone can accept.

If you have any latent family conflict—a shared property, unspoken expectations about who will care for parents when they age, a family business without a clear succession plan—the time to propose rules is now. Before the funeral. Before the crisis. Before emotions make rational conversation impossible. An imperfect rule agreed upon in advance is better than the absence of rules when everything explodes.

Beyond inheritances, families operate through coalitions that shift depending on the issue.

Two siblings might be allied against the third in the discussion about the house, but split differently when the topic is who takes care of mom on weekends. Cousins who can't stand each other discover they share a common enemy in an uncle who thinks he has the right to comment on everyone's life. In-laws who never got along suddenly cooperate because both want Christmas gatherings to be shorter.

The mistake is assuming permanent loyalties. The person who supported you last time might be on the other side this time, not through betrayal but because their interests changed or because the current issue affects them differently. Mapping these alliances before each major conflict—understanding who has what interests, who's aligned with whom on this specific issue—is valuable information most people ignore by assuming positions are fixed.

And then there are the annual negotiations that seem minor but accumulate resentment: where to hold the New Year's dinner, how to handle gifts when the family has grown too large, what to do with the relative who always ruins gatherings with hurtful comments or predictable drinking.

For divisions that repeat—where to spend each holiday, how to distribute care responsibilities, who organizes which event—there exists a simple principle that produces surprisingly fair results: one cuts, the other chooses. If two family branches take turns deciding where to celebrate, whoever decides this year knows they'll be on the other side next year. The incentive is to propose something reasonable, because the situation will reverse. The same principle applies to dividing tasks, rotating responsibilities, any resource that must be distributed repeatedly.

The problematic relative—the one who drinks too much, the one who makes incendiary political comments, the one who criticizes everyone's life choices—deserves their own strategy. Confronting them publicly usually escalates the conflict. Ignoring them allows the behavior to continue. The middle option is to establish boundaries without drama: sit far away, have a brief response prepared for predictable comments, accept that you won't change this person and minimize the damage they can cause in the hours you share space.

But there's a point where the best strategy is simply not to play.

Reducing exposure to toxic family dynamics is a valid option even though culture insists that "family comes first" and you must maintain relationships regardless of cost. If every family gathering leaves you emotionally exhausted, if interaction with certain relatives consistently damages you, if you've tried to establish boundaries and they've been repeatedly ignored, distancing yourself is legitimate protection.

This might mean attending fewer gatherings. It might mean going but leaving early. It might mean, in extreme cases, cutting contact with certain people while maintaining relationships with others. The obligation to maintain family ties has limits, and those limits are where your well-being is sacrificed without getting anything in return.

The difference between families that survive their conflicts and those that destroy themselves is rarely the absence of disagreements. All families have tensions, incompatible interests, moments where someone feels unfairly treated. What distinguishes those that endure is the existence of mechanisms to process those conflicts: agreed-upon rules for how decisions are made, channels to express discontent before it accumulates, willingness to renegotiate agreements that stopped working.

Families that survive aren't the ones that avoid conflicts. They're the ones with clear rules for resolving them.

23. Salary Negotiation and Interviews

Before you read any further, answer this honestly: if tomorrow they offered you the job you want but with a salary twenty percent lower than you expected, would you reject it? Do you have something better waiting if you say no? Or is the alternative to keep searching, with bills piling up and pressure mounting each week?

Your answer to those questions determines almost everything that will happen in the negotiation. Not your argumentative skills. Not your experience. Not how much you deserve that position by objective criteria. What defines your real power is one thing: how good your alternative is if this deal doesn't close.

There's a term for this worth knowing: BATNA, which stands for Best Alternative to a Negotiated Agreement. It's the option you have available if you walk away from the table and decide not to sign. It could be another job offer. It could be your current job, if you have one. It could be a period of searching funded by savings. Or it could be nothing concrete—just vague hope and growing anxiety.

The person who has a good alternative negotiates completely differently from someone who has none. The first can afford to ask for more, to reject terms that don't suit them, to take time to think. The second accepts whatever they're offered because anything is better than the void waiting if they say no. And most revealing: both attitudes show. The interviewer perceives who's negotiating from abundance and who from desperation, even if neither mentions it explicitly.

This means salary negotiation doesn't start when they ask how much you want to earn. It starts weeks or months earlier, when you decide whether you're going to build real alternatives or depend on a single opportunity.

Having another concrete offer transforms the conversation. Suddenly you can say, with complete honesty, that you need time to evaluate because you have options. You can mention, without it sounding like a bluff, that others are interested in you. The company that wants to hire you knows that if they don't offer something competitive, you'll go elsewhere. That pressure works in your favor without you having to do anything more than exist in a position of strength.

But even without a formal offer in hand, you can improve your BATNA. Keep conversations open with other companies, even if you're not actively searching. Cultivate relationships that could turn into opportunities. Be clear that you could work independently for a few months if necessary. Each of these options, though not perfect, moves you away from the scenario of total dependence where any offer seems better than nothing.

The other crucial ingredient is information. When you sit across from someone who negotiates salaries regularly, there's a brutal asymmetry: that person knows exactly what they pay for similar positions, what the approved range is for this role, how much they're willing to stretch if the candidate is worth it. You, probably, know none of that.

Closing that gap requires advance work. Platforms where employees share salary information from their companies exist precisely for this. Conversations with colleagues in your industry—uncomfortable but valuable—reveal ranges that would otherwise remain hidden. Recruiters who contact you for positions you're not interested in can give you useful data if you ask them directly what the compensation range is. Every data point you collect before sitting down to negotiate is an additional card in your hand.

With that information, you can avoid two opposite mistakes. The first is asking too little, revealing that you don't know your market value and leaving money on the table that you could have gotten. The second is asking for something so far from reality that the conversation ends before it begins. The right range is somewhere between both extremes, and only research tells you where.

About specific numbers: the previous chapter explored how the first number in a negotiation anchors the entire conversation. That principle applies with particular force here.

If they ask how much you expect to earn and you respond with a figure, that figure becomes the ceiling of what you'll get. The negotiation will revolve around that number, moving downward, not upward.

That's why, when you have to give a number, start higher than what you'd accept. Not absurdly high, but high enough that there's room to maneuver. If your real goal is seventy, ask for eighty. When they counteroffer at sixty-five and you "concede" to seventy-two, both sides feel they negotiated. You got more than the minimum you would have accepted. They feel they brought you down from your initial position. Everyone wins, though the only number that really mattered was the final one.

There's something many forget when negotiating employment: salary is just one component. The complete package includes elements that sometimes matter more than the monthly number. Vacation days. Remote work possibility. Schedule flexibility. Performance bonuses. The title that will appear on your business card and affect your next job search. Budget for training or conferences. Equipment they provide. Parking. Health insurance with different coverage.

When the company can't move the base number, they can often move these other elements. And for you, some of them may be worth more than a few thousand extra in salary. Three extra vacation days each year, over a decade, are weeks of life recovered. The ability to work from home two days a week eliminates hours of commuting and increases your quality of life in ways money can't buy. Negotiating the complete package, not just the main figure, is how you expand the pie instead of fighting over fixed portions.

And then there's silence. The most underestimated negotiation tool that exists.

When they make you an offer, your instinct is to respond immediately. Thank them, ask for details, start the counteroffer. But there's something more powerful: saying nothing. Simply staying silent for a few seconds, looking at the number as if you're evaluating it.

Silence is uncomfortable. The person across from you, trained to fill empty conversational spaces, will feel pressure to speak. And frequently, what they say to fill that void works in your favor. "Of course, there's some flexibility." "We could review the number if there's any concern." "What did you have in mind?" Each of those phrases opens doors that your silence created.

It's not about using silence as a manipulative tactic for eternal minutes. It's about resisting the impulse to respond immediately, giving yourself a few seconds to think, letting the other party wonder what you're thinking. In those seconds, sometimes, they gift you concessions you hadn't asked for.

The question you should ask yourself now, before your next negotiation, is simple. Write it down if it helps: What is my real BATNA today? Not the one you'd like to have, not the one you could build in theory, but the one that concretely exists if tomorrow they offered you something and you said no. And the second question, equally important: Is there anything I can do before sitting down to negotiate to improve that alternative?

Sometimes the answer is yes—you could contact that company that showed interest months ago, you could update your professional profile to attract more opportunities, you could explore the market even if you're not actively searching. And sometimes the answer is there's not much margin, and then at least you negotiate with open eyes, knowing exactly how strong or weak your real position is.

What you can't do is pretend you have alternatives you don't have. Desperation has a smell. But you also can't settle for a weak position without trying to strengthen it first.

You're not negotiating against the employer in front of you. You're negotiating against your best option if that employer disappears. Improve that option, and everything else changes.

24. Colleagues and Teams: Allies or Competition?

Your colleague asks for help with their project. They've been stuck for weeks on something you could solve in an afternoon. The question seems simple: do you help or not?

But the real question has layers that aren't obvious. If you dedicate your time and knowledge, what do you get in return? Maybe gratitude, maybe a stronger relationship, maybe a reputation as someone generous and collaborative. Or maybe something less pleasant: they submit the project as their own, your boss never learns of your contribution, and next time they come back expecting the same while they advance and you're left solving other people's problems.

And if you don't help, what happens then? You protect your time and your competitive advantage. But you also create distance. Maybe resentment. Maybe, when you need something, they'll remember you weren't available.

The right answer doesn't exist in the abstract. It exists only in the specific context of your work environment, who that colleague is, how your organization operates, what kind of game you're actually playing.

What makes workplace relationships complicated is that they operate on two levels simultaneously. On one level, you and your colleagues share objectives: you want the company to work, projects to succeed, the team to thrive. At this level, cooperation is obvious. One person's victory is everyone's victory. But there's another level, less visible and rarely mentioned in team meetings. Promotions are limited. Raises come from a finite budget. The recognition your colleague receives is recognition you don't receive. At this level, the relationship is competitive. Not because anyone is a bad person, but because the structure imposes it that way.

Navigating this duality without cynicism but without naivety is one of the least taught and most necessary skills for surviving in any organization.

There are places where those who help others most are the most valued. Collaboration is visibly rewarded. Bosses notice who unblocked someone else's project, who trained the newcomer, who shared information nobody asked for. In these environments, being generous is a winning strategy. Connectors rise, hoarders stagnate.

But there are other places where the dynamic is exactly opposite. Someone who helps too much is seen as someone without their own work, as an available resource to absorb what others don't want to do. Generosity is interpreted as weakness. Those who protect their territory and individual victories are the ones who advance.

The most costly mistake is assuming your environment works one way when it works the other. And the only way to know is to observe. Not what the corporate values hanging on the wall say, but what actually gets rewarded and what actually gets punished. Who got promoted last year and what behaviors they showed. Who was fired or marginalized and what they did differently. That observation should inform your strategy.

Reciprocity that works long-term has two components. First: concentrate your generosity on people who have the capacity and willingness to reciprocate. Not everyone can return favors of the same caliber. Someone in a position with access to information, decisions, resources, can reciprocate in ways that someone without that access simply cannot. This doesn't mean ignoring others, but it does mean being conscious of where you invest your social capital. Second: diversify. If your entire network of favors depends on a single person, you're exposed. That person can change jobs, can fall from grace, can simply forget about you when it suits them. Having relationships with people in different areas, different levels, different circles gives you redundancy.

In almost every work environment, there's at least one person who operates by different rules. Someone who systematically takes credit for others' work. Who says one thing in private and another in public. Who sabotages subtly to advance. Who lies about what happened when nobody else was present.

The natural instinct when facing this type of person is to confront them. Expose their lies. Defend yourself publicly. But direct confrontation with someone like this rarely ends well. These people are usually skilled at manipulating narratives, and an open confrontation can make you look like the difficult one, the one who doesn't know how to work on a team, the one who creates drama.

Protection strategies are less emotionally satisfying but more effective. Document everything in writing: the emails where you confirmed who did what, the file versions that show your authorship, the messages where you agreed on something the other person later denies. Involve witnesses when possible: if you're going to have an important conversation with someone you don't trust, find a way not to be alone, copy a third party on the email, mention in a group meeting what you agreed on privately. And resist the temptation to badmouth this person to everyone. Constant complaining makes you look obsessed and weakens your position. An occasional mention, at the right moment, to the right person, carries more weight than a hundred scattered complaints.

There's a persistent naivety about how organizations work. The belief that decisions are made in meetings where everyone presents arguments and the best one wins. That votes reflect impartial evaluations. That the formal process is the real process.

The reality is different. Important decisions are usually made before the meeting starts. What happens in the room is the formalization of what was already agreed upon in hallway conversations, informal lunches, previous calls where actors with power aligned positions. This isn't necessarily corruption or conspiracy. It's simply how humans make group decisions. Nobody wants to expose themselves publicly without knowing how others will react. Nobody wants to fight battles without having measured forces beforehand.

If you arrive at an important meeting without having spoken to key people beforehand, you've already lost. It doesn't matter how good your arguments are. Positions are fixed and votes are committed. The practical implication: invest time in preliminary conversations. Find out who has real influence over the decision that matters to you. Talk to those people first, understand their concerns, look for points of agreement. The meeting is where you harvest what you planted before.

Before closing, an exercise that can change how you navigate your environment. Think about the people you work with regularly and classify them into three categories. Reliable allies: people you know will support you, people you can count on. Direct competitors: people going after the same resources as you, whose advancement could mean your stagnation. Wild cards: people whose position isn't clear, who could go in any direction.

Most people never do this mapping explicitly. They act as if everyone were equal, deserving the same level of trust and the same strategy. But they're not. The information you share with an ally isn't the same as what you share with a competitor. The support you ask from one isn't what you expect from the other.

Once you have the map, adjust your behavior with each category.

The discomfort of thinking about your colleagues in strategic terms is real. Work would be simpler if you could fully trust everyone, collaborate without reservations, assume that goodwill will always be reciprocated. But ignoring the cooperation-competition duality doesn't make it disappear. It only makes you vulnerable to those who do see it and actively navigate it.

At work, nobody is completely an ally or completely a competitor. The art is in managing both simultaneously, without losing sight of either.

25. The Free Rider and the Tragedy of the Commons (When Everyone Loses)

The college group project. Five names on the cover page, one person working until three in the morning. The other four showed up for the final photo, added their names to the document, and everyone got the same grade. The professor never knew who did what. The one who worked swore they'd never accept a group like that again. Those who didn't work learned a different lesson: that the system allows you to benefit from others' effort without consequences.

If this sounds familiar, you've experienced firsthand one of the oldest problems of human cooperation.

The phenomenon has a technical name: the free rider. Someone who travels for free in a vehicle that others pay for and maintain. Who enjoys the benefits of collective effort without contributing anything. Who correctly calculates that their individual contribution is so small in the total that no one will notice their absence, but the benefit they receive is complete.

The free rider's calculation is impeccable from their individual perspective. If the group project will get done anyway because others will do it, why make the effort? If the building fee will be paid because most neighbors comply, what difference does it make if one doesn't pay? If the environment will be saved or destroyed regardless of what a single person does, why sacrifice?

The logic is solid. And if enough people apply it, everything collapses.

The coworker who systematically avoids difficult tasks, who always has an excuse when it's time to stay late, who shows up smiling to receive recognition when the project turns out well. The neighbor who never contributes to building improvements but enjoys the garden others maintain, the security others finance, the facilities others repair. The company that pollutes while its competitors invest in clean technology, taking advantage of the fact that the air belongs to everyone and the cost of dirtying it is spread among millions while the benefit of not investing in filters is theirs alone.

Each of these actors is doing what's rational from their narrow point of view. And each is contributing to destroying something they need to survive.

There's a related concept that extends this idea to a larger scale. Imagine a pasture shared by several ranchers. Each can bring their cattle to graze there. The grass belongs to everyone, which means it belongs to no one. Each rancher faces a decision: how many cows should I bring? If they bring one additional cow, they receive all the benefit of that extra cow. But the cost of feeding it, the wear on the grass, is distributed among all the ranchers. Individual benefit, collective cost. The rational decision is to bring more cows. The problem is that all the ranchers make the same calculation. Everyone brings more cows. The pasture is overexploited. The grass disappears. Everyone's cows starve.

This pattern appears in places you probably recognize. The office fridge that no one cleans because cleaning it benefits everyone but the effort belongs only to whoever does it. The meeting room that everyone uses and no one straightens up. The shared bathroom that mysteriously always needs paper and never has anyone to replace it.

Traffic works the same way. Each driver seeks their individual benefit: arriving quickly. Each chooses the shortest route. The result of thousands of individually rational decisions is a traffic jam where no one arrives quickly. The shared resource, the streets, degrades until it becomes useless precisely because everyone tries to exploit it to the maximum.

And at the largest scale, climate change. The atmosphere is the common pasture of all humanity. Each factory that emits pollutants receives the complete benefit of not spending on filters, while the cost is distributed among all inhabitants of the planet, present and future. Free rider logic applied at industrial scale. Each actor waiting for others to sacrifice their profits for the common good.

The question that naturally arises is whether there's a way out. Whether the structure of the problem inevitably condemns the shared resource to destruction. The answer is that yes, there are ways out, but none are automatic. All require conscious intervention to change the incentives.

One solution is privatization. If the pasture has an owner, the owner has incentives to care for it. They won't allow it to be overexploited because the loss would be theirs. The office fridge that no one cleans could be assigned to a specific person with clear responsibility. The parking area that everyone disputes could have assigned spaces. When something belongs to everyone, no one cares for it. When something belongs to someone, that someone protects it.

Another solution is external regulation. A third party with enough power to impose limits and punish those who violate them. The government that establishes fishing quotas to prevent the ocean from emptying. The building administration that fines those who don't pay. The boss who tracks individual contributions in group projects. Regulation works when there's real capacity to monitor behaviors and apply consequences.

The third solution is perhaps the most interesting: communities small enough that reputation matters. In a group of three people, it's impossible to hide. If you don't work, the other two know. If you don't pay, your neighbors look at you differently. If you pollute, your community points you out. Small groups can create social norms that work without formal regulation because the cost of violating them is social exclusion, and that cost is too high for most people.

This explains why group work functions worse the larger the group. In a team of two, the free rider can't hide. In a team of ten, they can disappear into the crowd. It explains why small buildings tend to be better maintained than enormous complexes. It explains why traditional communities, where everyone knows everyone, frequently manage shared resources better than anonymous societies of strangers.

The underlying principle of all these solutions is the same: make the cost of not contributing greater than the benefit of being a free rider. As long as being a free rider is the rational option, there will be free riders. Changing that equation requires conscious design of incentives.

In your own life, there probably exist common resources that are degrading. The shared space in your office. Household responsibilities in your home. The group chat where some always organize and others always benefit without contributing. The useful question isn't to complain about the free riders, who will always exist as long as the system allows them. The useful question is what rule you could propose that would change the incentives. What mechanism would make contributing more attractive than taking advantage. Who could be the responsible owner, or the regulator with authority, or how could you make the group small enough for social pressure to work.

When everyone can take but no one must care, everything eventually gets destroyed. Not out of malice, but by structure. The solution is never to appeal to the good will of free riders. It's to create clear rules or owners that change the game.

26. Mass Games: Voting, Auctions, and Social Media

Election day. Your favorite candidate is polling third in every survey, far behind the two frontrunners. You know they have no real chance of winning. You also know that between the two who can win, one seems acceptable to you and the other seems disastrous. The question you face in the voting booth is uncomfortable: do you vote with your heart for who you really prefer, knowing that vote probably won't change anything? Or do you vote with your head for your second choice, the acceptable candidate, to prevent the disastrous one from winning?

There's no universally correct answer. But there is a reality that many prefer to ignore: voting isn't just expressing a preference. It's participating in a game where your decision interacts with millions of other decisions, and where the final result can be very different from what any individual voter wanted.

The phenomenon is known as strategic voting, and it appears whenever the electoral system allows splitting the vote between similar options to benefit the opposite option. If a thousand people prefer candidate A over B, but five hundred vote for A and five hundred for a third candidate C who resembles A, candidate B can win with less real support than their combined rivals. The voters for A and C, added together, were the majority. But their inability to coordinate left both without representation.

This creates a genuine dilemma. Voting for who you really prefer is consistent with your values, but it can contribute to an outcome you detest. Voting for your second choice feels like betraying your preferences, but it may be the only way to avoid your worst scenario. The tension between expression and strategy has no easy solution, and those who tell you that you should always vote your conscience or that you should always vote strategically are oversimplifying something that's genuinely complicated.

What you can do is enter the game with your eyes open. Know that your vote doesn't exist in isolation. That the specific electoral system determines which strategies make sense. That sometimes prior coordination with similar voters can resolve the dilemma before reaching the booth.

Auctions present a different but equally counterintuitive trap. Imagine you're participating in an auction for an object whose real value you don't know. It could be a property, a contract, the rights to something. You make your best estimate of what it's worth and bid accordingly. Other participants do the same with their own estimates.

The winner will be whoever made the highest estimate. Think about what that implies. If there are ten participants and each independently estimates the object's value, the estimates will form a distribution. Some will be too low, some too high, some close to the real value. The winner, by definition, will be whoever was at the high end of that distribution. But being at the high end doesn't mean having been the most insightful. It frequently means having been the most wrong on the upside.

This is known as the winner's curse. The prize systematically goes to whoever most overestimated the value. And when they finally get what they bought, they discover they paid more than it was worth. They won the auction and lost money.

The defense against this curse is to establish your maximum limit before the bidding starts, when you can still think coolly. Once the auction begins, the adrenaline of competition distorts judgment. Each increment seems small compared to what you've already invested emotionally. The feeling that someone else will take what was almost yours clouds your calculation. The only reliable anchor is the decision you made before entering the game, when there was no pressure or immediate competition.

Social media is a third type of mass game, perhaps the most ubiquitous in contemporary life. Every time you post something, you're playing simultaneously with hundreds or thousands of people. Most are silent spectators. Some will react. A few will interact directly. And everything is recorded, visible, searchable.

Many people's intuition is to treat social media as private conversation. They post what they're thinking in the moment, respond emotionally to provocations, vent frustrations as if talking to close friends. But the reality is different. Each post is a signal sent to a massive and diverse audience. Your current boss can see it. Your future employer can search for it. Your clients, your colleagues, your family members, people you don't know but who might matter someday. The signal you think you're sending to your close friends is received by everyone else too.

Public fights on social media illustrate this clearly. When you argue with someone in a visible forum, the real dynamic isn't between you and that person. The dynamic is between each of you and the audience watching. What looks like a debate is actually a performance where both are trying to look good before spectators. Winning the argument matters less than seeming reasonable, informed, witty, or firm to those watching. The opponent is almost irrelevant. The audience is everything.

Understanding this changes how you participate. The question before responding to an attack isn't whether you're right, but whether responding makes you look better or worse to those observing. Sometimes silence projects more dignity than the most ingenious reply. Sometimes withdrawing from a degenerating discussion is the only way to avoid being splattered. The game isn't with your visible opponent. It's with everyone else.

There's one factor that makes social media particularly toxic in certain spaces: anonymity. When your name and reputation are linked to what you say, there's a cost to behaving badly. But when you can create an account without a real name, without a photo, without history, that cost disappears. There's no repeated game because there's no persistent identity. There's no reputation to protect because there's no reputation to lose.

The result is predictable. Anonymous spaces attract the worst behaviors precisely because the mechanism that normally disciplines social conduct is deactivated. People say things they would never say with their name attached. Aggression escalates because there are no personal consequences. Trolls thrive because their business model is impossible when they have something to lose.

This doesn't mean anonymity is bad in itself. Sometimes protecting identity is necessary to report abuses or express unpopular opinions without reprisals. But it does mean that the toxicity of certain spaces isn't accidental or mysterious. It's the direct result of eliminating the reputational cost of bad conduct.

Before your next post on any platform, it's worth asking yourself three questions. First: what signal am I really sending, not just the one I intend to send? Second: who among everyone who can see this actually cares? Third: given all that, is it worth posting? This isn't a call for permanent self-censorship or analysis paralysis. It's simply recognizing that each participation in these mass games has consequences that go beyond the immediate moment.

What connects voting, auctions, and social media is the same paradox. In each case, your individual behavior seems insignificant. One vote among millions. One bid among dozens. One post among thousands daily. The temptation is to act as if it didn't matter, as if you were invisible, as if the global result didn't depend on you. But the global result is exactly the sum of all those individual behaviors that seemed not to matter. Each vote counts because all votes are individual votes. Each signal on social media contributes to the general environment because the general environment is the sum of all signals.

In mass games, your individual action seems like a drop in the ocean. But the ocean is made only of drops.

27. Habits, Procrastination, and Your Future Self: Games with Yourself

It's ten at night. Tomorrow you have to get up early. Your body is asking for rest and your mind knows that eight hours of sleep is the bare minimum. But the episode ended at an interesting point. Just one more, you think. Forty minutes later, the next episode also ends on a cliffhanger. Just one more. At one in the morning you finally turn off the screen, eyes burning and with the uncomfortable certainty that someone will pay the consequences of this decision.

That someone is you. But not exactly the you who's making the decision now. It's a future version of you who doesn't exist yet, who has no voice or vote at this moment, who will suffer the exhaustion and mental fog without having been able to defend their interests.

You just played a game against yourself. And you lost.

There's something strange about how humans make decisions across time. Today's you and tomorrow's you share a name, body, and biography. In theory they're the same person. But in practice, they function almost like different players with opposing interests. Today's you wants immediate pleasure, comfort now, to avoid effort in this moment. Tomorrow's you wants to have slept well, to have saved money, to have exercised, to have avoided that difficult conversation that's now a crisis.

The problem is that when the moment to decide arrives, only the present you is at the table. The future you can't speak, can't negotiate, can't protect their interests. They're an absent player in a game where their fate is being decided.

Temporal inconsistency has a recognizable pattern. Today you promise that tomorrow you'll go to the gym. You mean it. You visualize the future you exercising, feeling good, progressing toward their goals. But when tomorrow arrives and the alarm goes off, something has changed. The you who promised no longer exists. The you who exists now is sleepy, cold, has a thousand reasons to postpone. Tomorrow, you think. Tomorrow for real. And the cycle repeats indefinitely because each morning there's a new present you who doesn't feel bound by the previous one's promises.

Procrastination works the same way. Today's you doesn't want to face the difficult task. You know that Friday's you will have to do it in a panic and under pressure. But Friday's you isn't here now, and today's you prefers the immediate comfort of avoiding the effort. When Friday arrives, that you inherits a problem they didn't create but must solve. The bill always comes. The question is who pays it and under what conditions.

Addictions take this pattern to its extreme. Each dose is a loan from the future that's repaid with interest. The immediate pleasure is real and tangible. The cost is distributed forward, diluted among many future yous who will each carry a small part of the destruction. The you who consumes today gets all the benefit. Those who come after pay collectively with deteriorated health, damaged relationships, lost opportunities.

If this sounds like the Prisoner's Dilemma we explored at the beginning of the book, it's because it is. Two players who could cooperate for a better outcome but end up betraying each other. Except here both players are you at different moments in time. The present you betrays the future you every time they choose immediate pleasure over long-term wellbeing. And the future you can't respond, can't punish, can't do anything except inherit the consequences.

The solution to dilemmas between players that we already know was to create credible commitments. Limit your own options so that cooperation becomes inevitable. The same principle applies here, except the commitment is with yourself.

Paying for the gym for a full year in advance changes the calculation. Not going is no longer just missing exercise; it's wasting money you already spent. Putting your phone to charge in another room before sleeping eliminates the temptation to check it one last time, because getting up to find it requires enough effort to activate resistance. Placing the alarm on the other side of the room guarantees that to turn it off you'll have to get out of bed, and once you're standing, the hardest battle is already won.

Each of these commitments works the same way: the you of the past arranges the environment so that the you of the present has fewer options to sabotage the you of the future. It's legislating today to protect someone who can't yet protect themselves.

Choice architecture expands this idea systematically. The question isn't how to strengthen your willpower, which is a limited and unreliable resource. The question is how to design your environment so that good decisions are easy and bad ones are hard.

Reducing friction toward what you want to do more means eliminating the steps between intention and action. Laying out your exercise clothes the night before. Having healthy ingredients already cut in the refrigerator. Putting the book you want to read in the place where you'd normally sit to waste time. Each obstacle eliminated increases the probability that the future you, in their moment of weakness, will take the right path simply because it's the easiest.

Increasing friction toward what you want to avoid means the opposite. Uninstalling apps that consume your time without giving you anything. Storing credit cards in an inconvenient place to reach. Not having in your house the food you know you shouldn't eat. Each additional step between impulse and action is an opportunity for resistance to activate and the impulse to dissipate.

Creating small immediate rewards means recognizing that the human brain discounts the future brutally. A small pleasure now weighs more on the scale than a large pleasure later. You can use this in your favor. After exercising, allow yourself something you enjoy. After completing the difficult task, a genuine break without guilt. The immediate reward associates the desired behavior with something positive, making it more likely to repeat.

There's something deeper in all this that goes beyond techniques. It's a shift in perspective about who your future self is.

Instead of treating them as an abstract version of you who can handle any problem you load onto them, consider them as if they were another person. Someone you care about. Someone whose interests deserve protection.

You wouldn't burden someone you love with unnecessary debts. You wouldn't take away hours of sleep they need to function. You wouldn't leave them unsolved problems that will grow into crises. You wouldn't bequeath them a body deteriorated by decisions you enjoyed and they'll pay for.

Tomorrow's you didn't choose the circumstances they'll inherit. Today's you can choose what circumstances to leave. That asymmetry of power comes with a responsibility that's easy to ignore because no one demands it of you, because the future you can't claim it, because the consequences will arrive when you no longer clearly remember the decisions that caused them.

Now think of a specific habit that your present self enjoys but your future self pays for. It could be staying up too late, postponing something important, spending on things you don't need, consuming something that gradually harms you. Identify it honestly. And then design a single commitment, just one, that makes the short-term option harder. Not a complete personal transformation plan. A single change in your environment that limits the present you's options to protect tomorrow's you.

Tomorrow's self has no voice in today's decisions. They can't vote, can't negotiate, can't defend their interests. Your job, as someone who does have power now, is to protect them even though the self of this moment protests. It's the strangest form of caring for someone: caring for someone who doesn't exist yet but who will inevitably exist and who will be you.

28. Most Common Mistakes and How to Avoid Them

You've read twenty-seven chapters. You understand what a Nash Equilibrium is, how the Prisoner's Dilemma works, why threats need to be credible, when it's best to anchor first in a negotiation. You have a new vocabulary for thinking about strategic situations and a framework to analyze them.

And still, you're going to make mistakes. We all do. Not because we're stupid or because we haven't understood the theory. But because in the real moment, under pressure, with emotions involved, abstract knowledge has the habit of evaporating just when we need it most.

What follows isn't new theory. It's a list of the most common ways we fail strategically, presented not as an academic catalog but as a practical warning. You'll probably recognize yourself in several. The hope is that next time you're about to commit one, something in your mind will raise an alert flag.

Forgetting you're in a game. You make a decision thinking only about what you want, analyzing only your options, considering only your preferences. You forget that there are other players whose reactions will affect the outcome. You choose the restaurant without considering that your partner also has preferences. You announce a policy at work without anticipating how those affected will respond. You raise prices without thinking about what your competitors will do. The result you get doesn't depend only on what you do, but on what everyone does in response.

Assuming everything is zero-sum. Someone has to win for another to lose, you think. Each concession of yours is a victory for the other, each gain of theirs is a loss for you. This mentality leads you to fight fiercely for every point, to defend positions to exhaustion. And meanwhile, the pie that both could have enlarged remains small because no one stopped to ask if there were ways to create more value before dividing it. The energy spent on division could have been invested in multiplication.

Ignoring the future. The deal that optimizes your result today can destroy a relationship that would have benefited you for years. Winning this argument with your partner can mean losing the trust that took time to build. Squeezing this supplier to the maximum can mean that next year they won't want to work with you. In repeated games, which are most of life's important games, sacrificing tomorrow for today is a losing strategy.

Making threats you won't follow through. You tell your child that if they don't clean their room there will be no dessert, and then you give them dessert because you don't want to deal with the tantrum. You tell your boss you'll quit if they don't improve your conditions, and both of you know you have nowhere to go. Each empty threat teaches the other party that your words mean nothing. Your credibility, once lost, is hard to rebuild. And without credibility, you have no negotiating tools.

Revealing information that hurts you. In the enthusiasm of a conversation, you tell the seller exactly how much you need that product. You tell the recruiter this is the only job you're interested in. You share with a competitor details of your strategy they had no way of knowing. This isn't about lying or being paranoid. It's about understanding that in strategic contexts, information has value, and giving it away without receiving anything in return is an unforced error.

Not calibrating your counterpart. You assume they think like you, that they value what you value, that they'll respond as you would respond. Or you assume the opposite: that they don't think at all, that they're irrational, that their actions have no logic. Both assumptions blind you. The person in front of you has their own interests, their own information, their own way of processing decisions. Your optimal strategy depends on how they really are, not on how you think they should be.

Escalating unnecessarily. A minor disagreement becomes an argument. The argument becomes a fight. The fight becomes a war. At each moment of escalation, responding with more force seems justified because the other just raised the tone. But the accumulated cost far exceeds what was originally at stake.

Two people end up not speaking over a comment that neither remembers clearly. Pride demands responding to each blow. Strategy asks you to calculate whether the response is worth its cost.

Overthinking. You calculate ten levels deep: I think that he thinks that I think that he thinks. You design sophisticated strategies to counter moves your opponent never considered. Meanwhile, your opponent is operating at level one or two, and your elaborate multi-level strategy leaves you worse off than if you'd acted with simplicity. Thinking one level above your counterpart is an advantage. Thinking eight levels above is a waste of energy that distances you from reality.

Eight errors. You've probably committed several this week. Me too. The difference between someone who improves over time and someone who repeats the same patterns isn't perfection. It's speed of recognition. Realizing mid-escalation that you're escalating unnecessarily. Noticing that you're assuming zero-sum without having verified it. Perceiving that your threat isn't credible before making it.

Now the personal question. Of these eight errors, which one is yours? Not the one you commit occasionally, but the one you commit systematically. The one that appears again and again in different contexts. The pattern you recognize yourself doing even though you know you shouldn't. Identifying it is the first step. The second is making it visible. A post-it on your desk, a note on your phone, something you see before making important decisions. Not as a sermon or as shame, but as a simple reminder of where you tend to fail.

Knowing the errors doesn't make you immune to them. You'll keep making them, though perhaps less frequently. What changes is the speed of correction. You recognize faster when you're falling into the pattern. You adjust before the damage is irreversible. And over time, the error that was automatic becomes increasingly a conscious choice you can avoid.

29. Seven Strategic Questions

You have an important decision in front of you. Maybe it's accepting or rejecting a job offer. Maybe it's confronting a partner about a financial disagreement. Maybe it's deciding whether to move in with your significant other or wait longer. The matter keeps you up at night. And obviously you don't have time to reread twenty-eight chapters looking for which concept applies to your specific situation.

What you need is a quick audit. A set of questions you can ask yourself before any strategic decision that force you to see what normally remains invisible.

There are seven questions. Learn them and they'll serve you for the rest of your life.

Let's walk through them using a concrete situation: you've been offered the chance to buy a stake in an acquaintance's business. The price seems reasonable, the opportunity interesting, and you need to decide in the coming days.

Who are the players? The obvious answer is you and the seller. But there are less visible players. If you have a partner, their financial preferences enter the game. If the business has other partners, their dynamics will affect you. If there are competitors in the market, their moves will determine part of the success. And there's a player almost no one includes in their analysis: your future self. The you five years from now who will live with the consequences of this decision, who has no voice now but will carry the results. When you map all the real players, the situation stops looking like a simple deal between two people.

What's really at stake? The superficial answer is money. But think deeper. Your time is at stake, because managing a stake requires attention. The relationship with that acquaintance is at stake, which will inevitably change when money is involved. Your reputation is at stake if the business fails, or if you withdraw in a way others consider disloyal. Your pride is at stake if the opportunity prospers and you didn't participate, or if you participate and it goes wrong. The money you invest is the visible part. The invisible frequently weighs more.

Is it zero-sum or is there potential for positive-sum? In buying a stake, it seems zero-sum: each dollar you pay is a dollar the seller receives, and vice versa. But look beyond the price. If your entry into the business brings knowledge or contacts the seller doesn't have, both can win more than existed before. If you structure payment in installments tied to results, you align incentives in ways that benefit both. Before negotiating each point hard, ask yourself if there are ways to create value that neither is seeing.

Is it a one-time or repeated game? If this acquaintance disappears from your life after the transaction, the rules are one thing. If you'll continue interacting, working together, seeing each other in social circles, the rules are completely different. In a repeated game, squeezing every advantage today can cost you future cooperation. The reputation you build in this negotiation will precede you in the next ones. The seller can accept a bad deal and hold a grudge for years. Or they can feel you treated them fairly and become a valuable ally.

What information does each party have? The seller knows details about the business you don't: hidden problems, difficult clients, real reasons why they're selling. You know things they don't: your true ability to pay, your alternatives, how much you really want this opportunity. Information asymmetry is the norm in almost every negotiation. Before acting, ask yourself what the other knows that you don't know, and what you know that you prefer to keep hidden. The answers to both questions should influence your strategy.

How can I make my promises and threats credible? If you say you can't pay more than a certain amount, is there something that makes that statement credible beyond your words? If you promise to get actively involved in the business, what signal can you give that demonstrates you're serious? Commitments that limit your own options—a deposit, a contract with penalties, a public declaration—make your position harder to ignore. Promises without cost are just words. Those that cost something are the ones others believe.

What's your BATNA? If this negotiation collapses, if there's no agreement, if you get up from the table and leave, what alternative do you have? Another investment opportunity waiting for you defines a very different position than this being the only train passing by. Your BATNA determines how much pressure you can resist, how much silence you can maintain, how much you're willing to risk. Before negotiating, ask yourself honestly what happens if you say no. And if that alternative is weak, consider whether you can strengthen it before sitting down at the table.

Seven questions. None require mathematics. None require specialized knowledge. What they require is honesty with yourself and willingness to see the complete situation, including the parts you'd prefer to ignore.

The power of this exercise is in doing it in writing. Not in your head, where answers remain vague and contradictory. Take a sheet of paper, write the seven questions, and answer each one for the decision you're facing right now. The act of writing forces you to be specific. It shows you the gaps in your analysis. It reveals what you thought you knew but didn't really know.

When you finish, you probably won't have the perfect answer. But you'll have something more valuable: clarity about what exactly you're deciding, who you're playing with, and what's genuinely at stake. With that clarity, the decision you make will be yours, informed, conscious of the risks.

You don't need to remember every concept from every chapter. You need to remember the right questions.

30. Infinite Games: When the Goal is to Keep Playing

A chess player sits down at the board with a clear objective: to win. There are sixty-four squares, thirty-two pieces, fixed rules. At some point, someone will deliver checkmate or concede defeat. The game will end. There will be a winner and a loser. The pieces will go back in the box.

Life doesn't work that way. There's no definitive checkmate. There's no moment where the game concludes and someone takes home the trophy. The only real "Game Over" comes at the end of everything, and by then the intermediate victories matter pretty little.

This distinction between finite and infinite games changes the application of everything we've discussed.

A finite game has clear rules, defined players, and an agreed-upon ending. Chess, an auction, an exam, an election. Someone wins, someone loses, everyone leaves. The strategy here is to maximize the probability of victory before time runs out.

An infinite game operates differently. There's no defined ending. There's no declared winner. The objective isn't to win but to keep playing. Your professional career works this way: there's no moment where you "won" your career and they hand you a trophy. Your health works this way: it's not about defeating your body but about keeping it operational. Your long-term relationships work this way: the goal isn't to beat your partner but to keep building something worthwhile.

The costly mistake is applying finite game logic to infinite game situations.

You win an argument with your partner. You demolished their arguments, proved your point, left them without a response. Technical victory. But they went to bed feeling ignored, and now they're questioning whether it's worth continuing to have these conversations with you. You won Tuesday night. You lost something that's not easily recovered.

A company maximizes profits this quarter. It cuts development, squeezes suppliers, burns out employees. The numbers look spectacular. But next year there are no new products, suppliers seek other clients, competent employees have left. The company won the quarter and compromised the next five years.

In infinite games, the useful question isn't "how do I win?" but "how do I keep playing in good conditions?" Sometimes that means deliberately losing specific battles. Conceding even when you're right. Sacrificing immediate gains to preserve future options. Accepting an inferior result today to maintain the relationship that will serve you tomorrow.

There's something else worth saying in this closing, and it's that strategic thinking has practical limits.

There are contexts where calculating too much ruins what you're trying to protect. If at every dinner with friends you're evaluating who paid what, who owes favors to whom, who initiated contact the last three times, your friends will probably start to feel the relationship has become transactional. And they'd be right. Excessive accounting kills the spontaneity that makes having friends worthwhile.

There are moments where the best move is to stop playing. To give something without calculating the return. To trust without having verified all the guarantees. To forgive without demanding compensation. Not because it's tactically brilliant, but because living in permanent strategic mode is exhausting and produces fragile relationships.

Those who optimize every interaction frequently end up alone or surrounded by people who are also optimizing. That sounds like a contradiction after twenty-nine chapters explaining how to think strategically. But the contradiction is only apparent.

The tools in this book are exactly that: tools. A hammer is for driving nails, not for solving every problem in your house. Strategic thinking is for situations where there are real conflicting interests, where others are calculating and you should do the same, where naivety leaves you exposed.

Use these ideas for negotiations where money or power is at stake. To protect yourself from people who manipulate without scruples. To understand why certain patterns repeat in your life and what you could do differently. To design agreements that work for everyone involved.

But don't turn every interaction into a strategic exercise. Don't analyze every conversation looking for hidden players and Nash Equilibria. Don't treat your family as counterparts in a permanent negotiation. There are spaces where what's appropriate is simply to be present without an agenda.

The real skill isn't applying game theory to everything. It's distinguishing when you're in a situation that requires strategic thinking and when you're in a space that works better without it. That distinction is worth more than any specific technique.

In the games that matter—your health, your close relationships, your long-term work—winning isn't the objective. The objective is to keep playing in reasonable conditions, with people who matter to you, doing things that are worth your time. Tactics that sacrifice that for specific victories are bad tactics, no matter how clever they seem in the moment.

THE END

Appendix 1. The 10 Most Useful Games

This appendix is for quick reference. When you face a situation and want to identify what type of game you're playing, check the table and then read the corresponding description. The correct diagnosis is half the solution.

GAME	YOU RECOGNIZE IT WHEN...	KEY STRATEGY
Prisoner's Dilemma	Both distrust and both lose	Communicate, create commitments, repeat the game
Stag Hunt	Big reward if they cooperate, risk if one fails	Build trust gradually
Game of Chicken	Neither wants to yield first	Offer the other a dignified exit

Zero-Sum	What one gains, another loses	Negotiate hard but fair
Positive-Sum	Both can win	Seek interests, expand the pie
Tragedy of the Commons	Shared resource gets destroyed	Create rules, owners, or community
Repeated Game	You'll see this person again	Tit for Tat: cooperate, respond, forgive
Asymmetric Information	One knows more than the other	Signal or seek signals
Coordination	Both want the same thing but don't know what the other will do	Seek focal point, communicate
Infinite Game	No defined end, the goal is to keep going	Prioritize relationship over victory

Prisoner's Dilemma. Two coworkers could collaborate and both look good, but each fears the other will take sole credit. Result: both work in silos, the project turns out mediocre, nobody wins. You recognize it because mutual distrust produces an outcome nobody wanted. The way out requires changing the conditions: communicate intentions explicitly, create verifiable commitments, or transform the one-time interaction into a repeated relationship where betraying today has costs tomorrow. If you can't change any of these things, at least go in with your eyes open knowing the other party faces the same perverse incentives you do.

Stag Hunt. Two partners could launch an ambitious business together, but each fears the other won't commit enough. If both bet big, the prize is large. If one bets and the other keeps their safe job "just in case," the one who bet loses everything. You recognize it because there's a valuable prize that requires simultaneous cooperation, and the main risk isn't that the other wants to betray you but that they don't trust enough to jump. The strategy is to build trust gradually: start with small bets, demonstrate commitment with costly signals, increase intensity as both verify the other is really all in.

Game of Chicken. A salary negotiation where neither wants to yield first. A couple's dispute where both wait for the other to apologize. A strike where company and union stare each other down. You recognize it because yielding feels like losing, but not yielding when the other doesn't yield either produces disaster for both. The temptation is to project that you'll go all the way, but if both do it, the crash is inevitable. The superior strategy is to offer the other a way to yield that doesn't feel like defeat. Reframe the situation so that moving first seems reasonable, not humiliating. The person who builds dignified exits usually gets better results than the one who simply shouts louder.

Zero-Sum. A fixed inheritance among three siblings. A single job position with multiple candidates. A negotiation where the price you pay is exactly the price the other receives. You recognize it because there genuinely is no way for both to win more: each additional dollar for you is one less for the other. Here it does make sense to negotiate firmly, defend your position, not give away value unnecessarily. But even in pure zero-sum, maintaining the dignity of the process matters if you'll interact with this person again. Winning by destroying the relationship can be worse than winning a bit less but preserving future options.

Positive-Sum. A couple discussing vacations. A work team defining how to divide responsibilities. Two companies exploring an alliance. You recognize it because both could end up better than at the start if they find the right structure. The common mistake is treating it as zero-sum and fighting over fixed positions. The strategy is to explore underlying interests before defending positions. Ask "why do you want that?" instead of assuming what they're asking for is what they really need. Look for ways to expand the pie before discussing how to divide it. The best positive-sum negotiations end with both parties feeling like winners because they found value neither saw at the start.

Tragedy of the Commons. The office refrigerator that nobody cleans. Traffic where each driver seeks their own benefit and everyone ends up stuck. The natural resource everyone exploits because nobody owns it. You recognize it because there's a shared resource that degrades precisely because it's shared: each person has incentive to use it and none to care for it. Solutions involve changing that structure. Assign clear ownership so someone has incentive to care. Create rules with real consequences for those who abuse it. Reduce the group to a size where social pressure works. Without some of these interventions, deterioration is inevitable even though nobody wants it.

Repeated Game. Your relationship with a regular supplier. With a colleague in your department. With the neighbor you'll see for years. You recognize it because you know there will be more future interactions, which changes the incentives of the present interaction. Cheating today has costs tomorrow. Cooperating today builds capital for later. The proven strategy is simple: start by cooperating, respond proportionally to what the other does, but always leave the door open to cooperate again if the other changes. Be predictable in your willingness to cooperate and in your willingness to respond if they fail you. The reputation you build in repeated games is one of your most valuable assets.

Asymmetric Information. The used car seller knows more about the vehicle than you do. The job candidate knows more about their weaknesses than the recruiter. Your negotiating counterpart knows how badly they need to close the deal. You recognize it because there's relevant information distributed unequally, and that asymmetry affects who has the advantage. If you know more, the strategy is to signal your value with actions that are costly to fake: warranties, verifiable references, commitments that only someone trustworthy would make. If you know less, the strategy is to seek signals, ask questions that reveal information, and be skeptical of words that cost nothing to say.

Coordination. Two people who want to meet but can't communicate and must choose where to go. Two companies that would benefit from using the same technical standard but neither knows what the other will choose. A group that needs to act in sync but without a clear leader. You recognize it because both parties want the same thing but the problem is coordinating, not competing. The strategy is to seek the focal point: the obvious option any reasonable person would choose in this situation. When you can communicate, do so explicitly. When you can't, choose the predictable over the creative. In coordination problems, originality is the enemy of success.

Infinite Game. Your professional career. Your health. Your long-term relationships. You recognize it because there's no defined ending where someone wins and the game ends. The goal isn't to win but to keep playing in good conditions. The strategy is to resist the temptation to optimize point victories at the cost of your ability to stay in the game. Don't destroy a relationship to win an argument. Don't sacrifice your health for a quarter's results. Don't burn your reputation for a tactical advantage. In infinite games, pyrrhic victory is the most common form of defeat.

Most real situations combine several of these games. A job negotiation can be positive-sum in the overall package, zero-sum in the specific salary number, a repeated game if you'll keep working with this person, and have asymmetric information about how badly each party needs to close the deal. The value of this classification isn't finding a perfect label but identifying what dynamics are operating and what strategies correspond to each one.

Appendix 2. Biases That Sabotage Your Decisions

In Chapter 3 we explored how emotions and biases interfere with strategic thinking. This appendix expands that discussion with the ten most relevant biases for decision-making in contexts where outcomes depend on others. Knowing them doesn't make you immune, but it does allow you to detect them before they cause too much damage.

1. Overconfidence

You overestimate your abilities, your information, and your chances of success. You underestimate obstacles, required timelines, and the competition.

Example: You decide to start a business without researching the market because you "know the industry." Six months later you discover there were three established competitors offering the same thing at a lower price. The information you didn't have was more important than the experience you thought you had.

Antidote: Before important decisions, actively seek reasons why you might be wrong. Ask someone who has no incentive to agree with you.

2. Loss Aversion

The pain of losing something weighs more than the pleasure of gaining the same thing. This makes you take asymmetric decisions: you risk too much to avoid losses and risk too little to obtain gains.

Example: You refuse to sell an investment that has lost value, hoping it will "recover," while you would have sold immediately if it had risen by the same percentage. The result: you hold losing assets too long and sell winners too soon.

Antidote: Ask yourself if you would buy today what you already own at the current price. If the answer is no, the fact that you already possess it shouldn't change the decision.

3. Herd Mentality

You assume that if many people are doing something, they must have information you don't have. You follow the crowd without verifying if the crowd knows where it's going.

Example: Everyone in your industry is adopting a new technological tool. You adopt it too, without evaluating whether it solves a problem you actually have. It turns out most adopted it because they saw others adopting it, and nobody did the original analysis.

Antidote: When you notice you're doing something "because everyone does it," pause and ask what independent evidence exists that it's a good idea.

4. Confirmation Bias

You seek information that confirms what you already believe. You ignore, minimize, or reinterpret information that contradicts it.

Example: You're convinced a colleague is unreliable. Every time they're late or make a mistake, you register it as evidence. Every time they deliver or help, you dismiss it as an exception. Your mental file is curated to confirm your initial belief.

Antidote: Deliberately seek information that contradicts your position. Ask yourself what evidence would make you change your mind, then actively look for it.

5. Anchoring Effect

The first number or piece of data you receive disproportionately influences your later estimates, even if that initial number was arbitrary or irrelevant.

Example: You see a product with a crossed-out price of two hundred and a sale price of one hundred twenty. You feel it's a good deal. If you had seen only the price of one hundred twenty without reference, you would have evaluated it differently. The anchor of two hundred distorted your perception of real value.

Antidote: Before receiving others' proposals, establish your own independent estimate. Have your number clear before someone gives you theirs.

6. Sunk Cost Fallacy

You continue investing in something because you've already invested so much, even though evidence indicates you should abandon it. The past you can't recover distorts decisions about the future.

Example: You've spent three years in a career you don't like. Each passing year, the idea of changing feels more costly because you've "already invested too much." But the time already spent won't come back regardless of what you do. The right question is whether the next three years are worthwhile, not whether the previous ones were wasted.

Antidote: Ask yourself: if I were starting from zero today, with no previous investment, would I make this same decision? If the answer is no, what you've already spent shouldn't change that.

7. Status Quo Bias

You prefer to keep things as they are, even when changing would improve your situation.

The effort of changing feels disproportionately costly compared to the benefit.

Example: You know you could get a better interest rate by switching banks, but you've gone years without doing it because it would involve paperwork. The real cost of switching is a few hours of forms. The cost of not switching is money lost every month for years. But inertia wins.

Antidote: Periodically ask yourself: if I weren't already in this situation, would I choose it today? If the answer is no, the fact that you're already there isn't sufficient argument to stay.

8. Availability Bias

You overestimate the probability of events you remember easily, usually because they're recent, dramatic, or emotionally impactful.

Example: After seeing news about a plane crash, you feel more afraid of flying even though the statistics haven't changed. The recent event is available in your memory, so your brain interprets it as more likely than it is.

Antidote: When you notice a recent event is influencing your risk assessment, look for actual frequency data instead of trusting what "comes to mind" easily.

9. Endowment Effect

You value things more simply because you possess them. The same object seems more valuable to you when it's yours than when it belongs to someone else.

Example: You have an old piece of furniture you don't use. If someone offered to buy it for what it's really worth, you'd refuse because it's "worth more." But if that same furniture were in a used goods store at the same price, you'd never buy it. Ownership distorted your perception of value.

Antidote: When evaluating something you own, imagine you don't have it and ask yourself how much you'd pay to acquire it. That figure is probably closer to the real value.

10. Future Discounting

You disproportionately value immediate rewards over future ones, even when waiting would produce much better results.

Example: You prefer to spend today on something that gives you immediate pleasure instead of saving for something that would give you much more value in a year. The future version of you who would benefit has no voice in the present decision. Today's you always wins the vote.

Antidote: Design commitments that limit your present self's options. Automate savings before seeing the money. Prepare the environment so the immediate option is also the right one long-term.

These biases aren't occasional errors but systematic patterns of the human brain. They evolved because they were useful in ancestral contexts, but they frequently fail in modern strategic decision situations.

You can't eliminate them through willpower. What you can do is create systems that counteract them: ask for a second opinion before big decisions, establish prior rules that limit in-the-moment discretion, actively seek information that contradicts your beliefs, and design your environment so the easy path is also the right one.

The effective strategist isn't the one who eliminates their biases, but the one who knows them well enough not to blindly trust their own perception.

About the Author

Diego Gómez studied Economics at UNAM and worked for several years in financial consulting in Mexico City. It was there he discovered that the best business decisions rarely depended solely on the numbers: they depended on anticipating what others would do.

That observation led him to study game theory, not as an academic discipline but as a practical tool. He eventually left the corporate world to dedicate himself to writing and teaching about strategic decision-making.

He currently lives in Los Angeles, where he works as a consultant and author. This is his first book on game theory applied to everyday life.

www.ingramcontent.com/pod-product-compliance
Lightning Source LLC
Chambersburg PA
CBHW060518100426
42743CB00009B/1359